THE MISERY MANIFESTO

A SELF-HELP GUIDE FOR THE SELF-ABSORBED

BARB BEST

THE MISERY MANIFESTO © copyright 2017 by Barb Best. All rights reserved. No part of this book may be reproduced in any form whatsoever, by photography or xerography or by any other means, by broadcast or transmission, by translation into any kind of language, nor by recording electronically or otherwise, without permission in writing from the author, except by a reviewer, who may quote brief passages in critical articles or reviews.

This book is a parody and has not been approved or authorized by the creators, authors, or representatives of any of the absolutely fabulous self-help and happiness books out there in the universe.

ISBN 13: 978-0-9833946-8-6
eISBN 13: 978-0-9833946-9-3

Library of Congress Catalog Number: 2016963143

Printed in the United States of America
First Printing: 2017

20 19 18 17 16   5 4 3 2 1

Cover design by Jessie Sayward Bright
Illustration Credits: Condé Nast, iStock Photo

Published by W.I. Creative Publishing,
an imprint of Wise Ink Creative Publishing.

W.I. Creative Publishing
837 Glenwood Ave.
Minneapolis, MN 55405
www.wiseinkpub.com

"Barb Best delights with a whole book full of reasons to be 'miserable.'"

—Anne Flournoy,
creator of comedy series *The Louise Log*

"Barb Best has artfully skewered the self-help industry while giving all of us access to her hilarious take on . . . well, everything. Hilarious!"

—W. Bruce Cameron,
New York Times bestselling author of *A Dog's Purpose*

"This satirical book about misery will make you . . . unmiserable! It's hilarious, witty, vivid, droll, and whip-smart. Contemporary, too, because Barb Best is up on the latest trends, tech, products, and pop-culture doings. This is your go-to book for laughing about love, sex, sleep, food, dogs, money, travel, and much more."

—Dave Astor,
humor columnist for the *Montclair (NJ) Times*, blogger at DaveAstorOnLiterature.com, and author of *Comic (and Column) Confessional*

"Barb Best makes misery an art form. Quoting from dignitaries that include the Buddha, Nietzche, and Kermit the Frog, she outlines a year of gloom, doom, and poop culture. Her witty words include the advice to stop exercising when your sports bra is so tight you bruise a rib when you cough. *The Misery Manifesto* proves that being chipper and Pollyanna-perky pisses people off, so read it soon before the world ends."

—Elaine Ambrose,
award-winning author of *Midlife Cabernet*

"Sixty minutes of thinking of any kind is bound to lead to confusion and unhappiness."

—JAMES THURBER

"Life is divided into the horrible and the miserable."

—WOODY ALLEN

[Right after smashing Paul's ankles with a sledgehammer] "God, I love you."

—ANNIE WILKES, played by Kathy Bates in the film *Misery*

TABLE OF CONTENTS

INTRODUCTION
ODE TO MISERY • 1

JANUARY
ENERGY CRISIS • 5

FEBRUARY
HEARTBURN • 19

MARCH
DRUDGERY AND PAIN • 33

APRIL
FISCAL FOLLY • 47

MAY
SICK AND TIRED • 57

JUNE
LONELINESS • 69

JULY
POOP CULTURE • 83

AUGUST
CHAOS • 97

SEPTEMBER
LITTLE MONSTERS • 109

OCTOBER
TECHNOLOGY HELL • 123

NOVEMBER
SLOTH • 133

DECEMBER
XTREME HOLIDAY STRESS • 143

CONCLUSION
THE MISERY MANIFESTO • 152

INTRODUCTION

ODE TO MISERY

> "Philosophers, scientists, saints, and charlatans all give instruction on how to be happy, but none of this matters to a person who doesn't want to be happy."
>
> —GRETCHEN RUBIN,
> author of *The Happiness Project*

There are a zillion "happiness" and "how-to-be-happy" self-help books out there. I find them depressing! These ☺ experts are so self-absorbed and serious they make me laugh.

A systematic, cerebral approach to happiness is like an academic probe of humor—it kills the golden goose. There's no fun in self-improvement prattle, analysis ad nauseam, and schmaltzy affirmations.

Why embark on a "thoughtful, engaging, and compelling" pursuit of happiness when bitching and moaning works wonders for your lousy mood? Lots of people thoroughly enjoy being miserable!

News flash to the happiness gurus: being chipper and Pollyanna-perky pisses people off, whereas misery loves company. It's where the cool kids are hooking up. Nothing's more satisfying than a down-and-dirty pity party.

Angst: it's a coping strategy. Misery: it's an art form. Complaining: it's a way of life if you do it right. Knock yourself out.

Let's face it: life is one long, dusty Via Dolorosa. The world gives us colossal migraines and substantial rectal aches. People are flawed, foolish, and self-involved. Life is messy and painful. Most times, it can be downright ridiculous. You might as well embrace the dirty, awful truth and laugh at your misery. You will experience the transformative power of humor. It will set you free.

This is my cockamamie prescription for happiness.

I feel your pain.

Enjoy!

INTRODUCING...
THE PILL-OF-THE-MONTH CLUB!
JANUARY
PROZAC
Winter Doldrums
FEBRUARY
VIAGRA
Valentine Vigor!
MARCH
CLARITIN
Hay Fever
APRIL
EXTRA-STRENGTH TYLENOL
Tax Time
MAY
ROGAINE
The Rites of Spring
JUNE
DEXATRIM
Bathing-Suit Season
JULY
EXCEDRIN
Kids Home a Lot
AUGUST
XANAX
Flying Somewhere?
SEPTEMBER
RITALIN
Back to School!
OCTOBER
ESTROGEN
Autumn Blues
NOVEMBER
ZANTAC
Turkey, etc.
DECEMBER
VALIUM
Holiday Overload
R. Chast

JANUARY

ENERGY CRISIS

"Every day starts, my eyes open, and I reload the program of misery.
I open my eyes, remember who I am, what I'm like, and I just go, 'Ugh.'"

—LOUIS C. K.

Blue

According to the misery index, "Blue Monday" is considered to be the most depressing day of the entire year. Blue Monday is in January. It is either the first, second, third, or fourth Monday—take your pick. Perhaps, for you, it is all of the above.

The misery index is calculated using various factors such as inflation, unemployment, horrible weather, high level of debt, low motivation, crippling disappointment over resolutions already broken, the cruel fact that the holidays have passed, the scarcity of eggnog, and tight underwear. You get the blue picture.

Think of it this way: January is the Blue Monday of months. Welcome to thirty-one days of unmitigated despair and melancholy.

After all, how productive can a month or year be when it begins with a daylong hangover, alarming weight gain, the prospect of an onerous diet and exercise regimen for the foreseeable future, and an avalanche of credit card debt from six weeks of highly focused holiday binging?

Short on Vitality? Out of Gas?

"OMG—I'm so tired!" If you're like me, you say this at least fifty, sixty times a day.

Damn it, where's a bottle of Vitameatavegamin when you need it?

"Lucy! We got a beeg problem!"

BTW, you probably have lots of gas but are still chugging around on low energy.

So, what to do?

Lower the bar. You heard me. Don't squander that last surge of energy from your fifth cup of Joe to go—God forbid—exercise. This requires much more than meets the bloodshot eye.

Exercise can drain you faster than a phone call from your aging mother.

To exercise, you have to locate your workout clothes, apply makeup in a manner that makes you look like you're not wearing makeup (you never know who you might meet), drag yourself to the car, drive to said gym, socialize while there, look like you're sincere about this whole fitness thing, and check out everybody else in their sexy spandex. (Most of them are younger than you and all are thinner.)

Then, you have to trudge home, first making an emergency stop at a fast-food joint to eat something, anything, before you die of a blood sugar crash.

Exercise has a sneaky way of making you inordinately hungry. After stuffing yourself silly, you still need to get home, change out of your stinking workout outfit, take a shower, wash your hair, apply makeup (so it looks like you're wearing makeup), and take a long nap.

Oy! This is way too much effort.

Tip for the Tired: Slacker Goals = Less Pressure

As relationship expert and best-selling author Margaret Paul, PhD, writes at *HuffPost* Healthy Living, "While life is often challenging, lonely, and heartbreaking, misery is a choice."

Hmmm. "Life is often challenging, lonely, and heartbreaking." Thank you! That's comforting! That's right up there with "Life's a bitch, then you die." Knit it on a pillow. Paste it on your vision board. Tatt it on a perky body part.

WAKE UP & SMELL THE CAFFEINE

Drip. Drip. Drip . . .

Random Thoughts after Five Cups of Coffee

If caffeine were an illegal drug, we'd all be in jail.

If we were all in jail, who would pick the beans and brew the coffee?

Federal prisons may be the only buildings in the world that don't have a Starbucks in the lobby.

What is "peace of mind" to me? A Keurig coffee maker with plenty of French Roast Dark on hand and Nespresso on tap.

Caffeine is jet fuel for the liftoff challenged and the terminally foggy.

Coffee beans, coffee beans,
They're good for your heart.
The more you gulp and guzzle,
The more you dart and dart and dart.

Crack is whack, but coffee is whee!

Hopped up on caffeine? Feel like a homicidal junkie on house arrest? There's help. Join CA—Caffeineholics Anonymous—where you can get the support you need, plus lots of cheap wine.

Advice: If you really want to be miserable, take a break from coffee—not a coffee break.

THE DEPRIVATION DIET

Eating healthy is harder than it looks. And it looks pretty nasty. Seriously, kale chips? Dried mango slices? Sardine paste on a jicama stick?

Rice "cakes" is a misnomer. It ain't rice, and it definitely ain't cake. Could be

Styrofoam. Definitely not fit to digest; however, rice cakes do make excellent packing material for recycled holiday gifts.

WTF is a legume? Nobody knows for sure. Animal? Vegetable? Mineral? My guess: alien space dropping.

Are you keen on quinoa? Who is truthfully in love with quinoa?

Love and passion should be preserved for key lime pie, chocolate fudge brownies, fettuccine Alfredo, and David Beckham. Methinks orgasms aren't the only thing women are faking!

AU NATUREL

Vegan? Vagan?
You say vee-gan, I say vay-gan,
Vee-gan, vay-gan,
Vee-Vay,
Oy vey,
Let's call the whole thing off!

You've seen those anemic-looking, ghostly souls who shadow us rosy-cheeked, robust (okay, rotund), marbleized meat gobblers? You know, the bird-boned wisps of women who resemble fashion models and meth addicts? Guess what, honey? Protruding shoulder blades are not sexy unless you're a praying mantis in heat.

You've got to feel for these waifs, with their spindle legs and trim waistlines. They live on kidney beans and alfalfa sprouts. They dine at natural food restaurants, just as I did recently. A restaurant with a name that's as conspicuously unpretentious as "Angel's Nook," "Moonbeam's Kitchen," or "Raw Delight" can't possibly excite my palate.

As you enter the retro kitchen klatch, it smells like a feed store or a colonic emporium. Regardless of the strong stench, which reminds you of the summer your cat battled colitis (unsuccessfully), the hostess is all wan smiles.

Good thing. You can quietly barf or expel gas (puh-lease only if absolutely necessary) and not a soul will even notice. Those aromas blend in perfectly with the entrees.

The menu is handwritten on recycled paper. Yes, there is a calico border. The selections read like a foreign language to the average American diner: bok choy, tatsoi, umeboshi paste, mesclun greens, lacinato kale, collards, and caramelized shiitake. Ugh. Gag me with a chopstick.

After being served a dog bowl of tofu-kale-quinoa-beet salad, I have deep regrets. Smack! "I could have had a V-8, or better yet, an In-N-Out" double-double cheeseburger with extra fries and a chocolate milkshake!"

One more bite of the split chickpea soufflé, and this wannabe vegan is craving pig slaughter videos.

BARB BEST

WHEN TO STOP EXERCISING!

PSST! We all know when to start exercising (right this minute), but here's when to stop.

1. You're starting to sweat like a camel in heat—if this keeps up, you might need to take a shower. Geez, this would require even more energy.

2. You're turning red, white, or blue—or all three—and it's not even the Fourth of July or—God forbid—an election year.

3. Your sports bra is so tight you bruise a rib when you cough.

4. Your thighs are chafing so much they start a brushfire in your tights.

5. Your trainer is screaming at you to forget "this crazy fitness thang."

6. Your feet have gone numb and your toenails are splitting off.

7. The elastic waistband on your spandex pants is causing kidney cramps.

8. Your earbuds have melded into your ear canals.

9. You're having a f*#!ing heart attack. Quick, pop an aspirin!

10. You're so ravenous you can't wait to wolf down a dozen frosted, fire-engine red

velvet chocolate cupcakes. So what if cupcakes are passé?

HAVE A F*#! IT LIST, NOT A BUCKET LIST

The trick here is not to have a long, tedious list of things you feel you want or have to do, but a list of tasks never to do. Very liberating.

25 Things I Don't Wanna Do Before I Croak!

1. Have my hard drive crash, thus losing decades of cherished family photo albums and irreplaceable cat videos.

2. A lumbar puncture. There doesn't exist a painkiller potent enough to make this procedure tolerable, let alone pleasurable.

3. A fiscal colonoscopy by the IRS.

4. A taste tour of Malaysian food stalls and rat-infested street bazaars with Andrew Zimmern, oafish host of the Travel Channel's Bizarre Foods. Call me unadventurous, but I've got zero hankerings for his brand of "gourmet" food: goat gonads tartare, fried scorpion nuts, and snake snot on a stick. Yuck it, dude.

5. Wear Pugnacious Purple incessantly. This color looks great on the California Raisins, but not on me! The tiniest blemishes—especially those on the face, neck,

and ankles due to errant veins and capillaries—will pop like fireworks in the blackest night.

6. Sleep with Mick Jagger. Such an ill-advised tryst would result in a case of multiple whiplash caused by his colossal . . . wrinkles.

7. Sit through one more moronic male buddy comedy.

8. Clean out that weird mess embedded in the bottom drawer of the fridge.

9. Lose that elusive five (okay, fifteen) pounds.

10. Take a selfie with a D-list celebrity.

11. Swim from Cuba to the Florida Keys. Diana Nyad, get a life.

12. Master the Macarena.

13. Learn Mandarin.

14. Rub elbows or knees with any of the Kardashians.

15. Wear a sleep bra.

16. Read a history of sock puppets.

17. Get excited about the latest celebrity hairstyles (exception: Lady Gaga).

18. Savor the subtle hint of hot sauce in Al Roker's artichoke dip.

19. Cuddle an armadillo.

20. Be stalked by TMZ—especially if I'm sans makeup.

21. Embrace hip hop. "Yo, yo, bitch."

22. Pretend I'm remotely interested in NFL picks, lingerie football, or ice hockey brawls.

23. Watch another cutesy car insurance commercial.

24. Boohoo over spilled soymilk.

25. Regret missed planes, bad luck, false friends, and lost loves.

AFFIRMATIONS FOR THE MISERABLE

Affirmations shouldn't be just for the lighthearted souls among us or for those busy bees tediously aspiring to be oh so merry. Here are some affirmations for the rest of us.

Wash. Rinse with tears. Repeat.

- I start each day with alcohol, sugar, and caffeine cravings.

- Life is a cabaret . . . too bad I'm tone deaf.

- The cat mocks me. Life is cruel.

- I choose indecision and despair over action.

- I nourish my inner bitch.

- There exists no trace of the happiness hormone oxytocin in my bloodstream.

"Not tonight, honey, but here's a voucher."

FEBRUARY

HEARTBURN

"Misery no longer loves company.
Nowadays it insists on it."

—RUSSELL BAKER

February is so punishing that every four years the powers that be feel the need to add a bonus day. Leap years give you an extra twenty-four hours to leap off the nearest bridge . . . if you're so inclined.

VALENTINE'S DAY PRESSURE

Valentine's Day: you either love it madly or despise it fully—no middle ground here.

Holidays, especially those steeped in romance, are all about expectations. Can we live up to our special tormentor's notion of a perfect evening/day/night/six-and-a-half minutes? Will our greedy little material, culinary, and erotic fantasies be fulfilled?

Report Card

Dear Connor,

Enclosed is your annual Valentine's Day evaluation. Comments will address key aspects of your holiday performance. When germane, I will reference concerns regarding the general progress you're making in our relationship.

- ✓ You receive above average marks on maintaining a positive attitude for most of the evening. We'll forgive (but not forget) the grumbling under your breath when I sweetly requested you serenade me with "Feelings."

- ✓ You demonstrated initiative and creativity (albeit with constant prodding and direction) by making plum restaurant reservations for the mandatory romantic dinner. You exceeded expectations by donning the sexy pink "lovebirds" necktie I gave you. ☺

- ✓ You enthusiastically participated in the consumption of the extravagant meal and (especially) the drinking of the inordinately overpriced French champagne. (Yes, I know you have suits that cost less than that measly bottle, but it was gauche of you to mention that while ordering.)

- ✓ Needs improvement: It is acutely evident that you need to work on developing greater concentration skills (soup spoons are not percussion instruments) and becoming a better listener ("What? Huh? What did you say? Huh?").

- ✓ You really should not require repetition to retain such basic information as my profound feelings about cocker spaniel puppies and deep thoughts on saving the planet from the calamity of cow flatulence.

- ✓ Your menu choices were a tad predictable (if not pedestrian) and mucho heavy on the garlic (spaghettini, really!). Additional food note: Spinach is never a wise idea on a date. You know why.

- ✓ You score big points for ordering a decadent dessert for us to share, then letting me wolf down the whole thing by myself—bravo! (I'll forever cherish the memory of that heart-shaped, Cointreau-laced, triple-dark cocoa crème mousse cake. Oh. My. God!)

- ✓ Gift giving: Frankly, this is an area where I'd like to see significant improvement. I encourage you to fulfill your potential and aspire to a much higher level. A VaJazzle kit is not an appropriate Valentine's Day gift for a woman of my substance—even though you steadfastly insist it was a joke.

- ✓ Please remember, there's *nothing*—nada, zip, zero, *nothing*—funny about Valentine's Day. This is serious business, Mister!

- ✓ Gold Star: I want to commend you for admiring the gift of fine jewelry I purchased for myself with your Visa Platinum card. If you work hard on your organizational skills, I have reasonable confidence you'll be able to handle this task yourself at some point.

- ✓ Flowers: The red roses were okay, but you neglected to remove the price sticker from the crappy grocery store wrapper. FYI—straight men are allowed inside florist shops.

- ✓ Embrace your metrosexual side and put a clamp on those (homophobic?) tendencies to avoid all things pink, pastel, and remotely "namby pamby," as you put it. Yellow ribbons and coral orchids never hurt anyone.

- ✓ Chocolate: Below-average marks. Hershey's Kisses are kibble for runny-nosed kindergarteners, not aphrodisiacs strong enough to kindle the loins of your beloved. Godiva has a website that offers double-cream gourmet truffles, plus emergency delivery. (And they *love* Visa Platinum.)

- ✓ Kudos! You excelled in the demonstration of physical affection. You get an A+ for effort. This is a strength you obviously take pride in. I encourage you to work on this critical skill set, and I'm happy to tutor you anytime.

- ✓ Plays well with others: (see "demonstration of physical affection").

I'm happy to have you in my relationship this year and look forward to increasingly rewarding times together.

Hugs and kisses from your loving girlfriend and biggest fan,

Kimberly

P.S. My birthday is five weeks away. I'm sure you'll rise to the occasion.

LOVE & SEX: WHY BOTHER?

There's a common bad dream (more like a night terror) that aspiring overachievers like you experience frequently: You're stark naked in a public place. You have a do-or-die test coming up. And, of course, you're seriously *un*prepared.

Now imagine this test is not on quadratic functions or Greek literature, but on your sexual performance.

Sweating? Heart racing? Toes tingling? Are we having fun yet?

Many people, male and female, experience performance anxiety. There's no cure.

Conventional wisdom suggests you face your anxiety head-on. Go on. Suck it up. Breathe hard. Have a couple bottles of vino, then go for the gold. With all the crazy panting going on, your partner won't notice you're hyperventilating.

Trust moi, the French know best on this affair: C'est la vie. Have a croissant.

YOU DON'T GET ENOUGH

If you're male, you don't get enough sex.//
But, who's counting?//
Oh . . . *you* are.

CHOCOLAT, MON AMOUR

If chocolate is the love of your life, you're not alone. You'll revel in February's dedication to filling the coffers of the dastardly, billion-dollar cacao cartel.

I personally dip *everything* in warm, luscious, bittersweet dark chocolate whenever I have a flame handy. There's often an old flame around if you look (try Facebook).

Studies have shown that there is something in the female brain (the C spot?) that reacts more positively to ingredients in chocolate than clumsy advances from your average adoring caveman.

By 2019, the world cocoa market is expected to be worth about $2.1 billion, and the world chocolate market is expected to be worth about $131.7 billion. That's a lot of Tootsie Rolls.

GREAT REASONS NOT TO HAVE SEX

1. You have a headache. No, a migraine.

2. You're busy giving someone else a headache.

3. You feel nauseated.

4. You didn't study.

THE MISERY MANIFESTO

5. Dog needs to go out.

6. You're focusing on texting and tweeting hilarious selfies.

7. You have low T.

8. You have high E.

9. You're worried about climate change.

10. Dog is hungry.

11. You haven't scheduled it on Outlook.

12. You reek of garlic.

13. He reeks of turkey jerky.

14. You have to condition your hair.

15. Dog wants to play.

16. There's a compelling reality TV show on.

17. You're still angry about (insert whatever).

18. You're stuck to your laptop.

19. You're sick to your stomach. Too much chocolate.

20. Dog ate some of your chocolate. You're rushing him to the vet.

LOVE STORY

You love your dog.
Your dog loves you.
He sleeps on your bed with you.
You enjoy long walks together.
You take car rides and beach trips together.
You share your food with him, especially meat and ice cream.
You believe deep in your heart that he's your soul mate.
He understands and respects your moods.
He's ever attentive.
He lives to please you.
Forget that you had him neutered early on in your relationship. He doesn't hold a grudge. He's above that sort of pettiness.
He's easygoing.
He's *so* sweet. There isn't a mean bone in his body.
He even plays the piano and serenades you. For this, he makes a nice chunk of change on YouTube and gives it all to you.
What a prince!
Oh, that's his name . . . Prince.
And he happens to be a hunky white Labrador retriever.

Should you marry him?

INTIMACY CHECK

Are You TOO "Up Close and Personal" with Your Smartphone?

8 Warning Signs

1. You can't take your hands off your phone.

2. With a camera (what's that?), you take pictures of your cell phone not wearing a case.

3. You run away to Vegas and marry your smartphone. A Los Angeles man did just that in August 2016. It is said to be his longest, most fulfilling relationship.

4. Your bumper sticker says, "My smartphone is smarter than your smartphone."

5. You panic if you momentarily think you left your cell at home.

6. If you—OMG!—actually leave your phone somewhere, you experience disturbing withdrawal symptoms and require emergency medical attention.

7. If you lose your phone, you need grief counseling.

8. Like Kim Kardashian, you take roughly one selfie a minute. This isn't just narcissism, it's indecent exposure. Go to jail and do not collect $200 million.

AFFIRMATIONS FOR THE HEARTBURNED

- Love . . . who needs it?

- Dark chocolate is my only friend.

- I attract people in pain.

- I kiss the sizzle in my sex life bye-bye.

- The shadow of your creepy smile sears my memory.

- My heart is open wide to chronic inflammation.

"Relax, and just try to imagine you're on a sunny beach."

MARCH

DRUDGERY & PAIN

"Misery is almost always the result
of too much thinking."

—JOSEPH JOUBERT

March Madness

T. S. Eliot was wrong. April is not the cruelest month; March is.

I've noted that most people are in a nasty rage the entire month of March. They're still grieving the end of football season. They're angry winter isn't yet over—"Jeez, it's still snowing!" They're angry they have to at least consider paying their taxes next month. March is just one long, pissy pity party.

The Misery Molecule

Scientists say they've found the brain's "misery molecule." It's believed to be responsible for all our feelings of stress and anxiety. We'll call it the M-Spot.

The M-Spot is the converse of the G-Spot.

The popular phrase "Out, damned spot!" was likely inspired by the M-Spot.

A stain remover for the M-Spot has not yet been invented, so most people use vodka or Vicodin. Family-sized bags of Peanut M&M's are also effective. Alas, these are short-term solutions that harm your happy molecules, distort your DNA, and eventually cause more pain than the initial problem.

The misery molecule is actually a protein called CRF1. It's found in the brain's pituitary gland (or as I call it, the "pity-ary" gland). The hypothalamus, a portion of the brain that produces feckless, mood-altering hormones, is involved—so we know nothing good will come of this interaction. (Can you spell P-M-S?)

Hormones! It all boils down to those pesky little biochemical mischief makers pranking our states of mind and influencing our behavior.

"Out, damned spot!"

Work, Work, Work

Who the hell said, "It's not work if you enjoy what you're doing."

Nonsense! If it eats the clock, burns calories, and shortens my life . . . it's work.

Even sleeping can be work, especially if you have one of those dreadful Fitbits or CPAP machines. Chances are if you must measure, record, and analyze it, it's work.

Cooking Is Work

Cooking, if you do it right, is a lot of work.

It is not an exciting sports competition, a fun game at the county fair, or a serene day at an East Hampton spa with your gay friends. Don't swallow that sugarcoated BS from the Cooking Network, the Food Network, the insatiable billion-dollar media conglomerates, and Rachel F-ing Ray.

It's a lot of schlepping, straining, stirring, standing, and sweating.

It requires heavy lifting and heavy metal.

Let's face it: cooking is two hours of stewing, heating, and corkscrewing for ten minutes of chewing.

Did I mention dishwashing and the big cleanup?

Remember: God made restaurants so we don't have to cook all, serve all.

But apparently tossing a frozen dinner into a microwave or picking up a greasy pizza at the local Cholesterol Café no longer qualifies as cooking to the new generation of "foodies."

DEAR FOOD NETWORK

Thank you for teaching my kids how to cook fancy-schmancy.

The vast culinary knowledge they've acquired lounging in front of the TV and laptop (love your website) has raised the chow bar to an unduly sophisticated level.

Unfortunately, they leave 99 percent of the actual cooking to moi.

I can no longer pawn turkey hot dogs, tuna sandwiches, or cans of chicken noodle soup off as a meal.

They expect me to produce gourmet cuisine in the ten minutes I have between finishing work and chauffeuring them to soccer-lacrosse-baseball-cheerleader-band practice.

They demand extraneous stuff like orange zest on their Greek yogurt and maple glaze on their friggin' Cheerios.

They now require more "complex flavors" in their lousy lasagna. Puh-lease!

They expect seven-tiered red velvet birthday cakes with homemade (my home!) ganache, raspberry filling, and f*!ing fondant.

They critique my plating skills, for God's sake!

Wonder why there's an obesity epidemic?

Duh! Maybe it's all that butter, cream, and sugar? I'm talking to you, Ina Garten, Duff Goldman, and Guy "Fatso" Fieri!

The latest lure is Kids Baking Championship, where tween chefs compete by creating gourmet dishes that would shame your favorite five-star restaurant.

Personally, I'm not prepared to blowtorch bell peppers or ramekins of crème brûlée in my crappy little kitchen.

I don't own restaurant-grade appliances. I wouldn't know an industrial ice cream maker or compressor from a Crock-Pot.

Enough with all the brining, caramelizing, deglazing, and clarifying!

Maybe I'll walk in to fix breakfast tomorrow a.m. and learn I've been chopped?

One can only hope.

FOOD FIGHT

Ready for Vegan Rehab?

I confess to playing around lately—with my food, that is. I'm flagrantly flirting with a macrobiotic diet.

MACROBIOTIC. Ahem. We all know macro means "large" and bios refers to "life." But is eating macrobiotic actually "living large"?

The macrobiotic diet consists of *whole* grains, *raw* vegetables, *unadulterated* fruits, legumes (whatever they are), and lots of fresh green plant leaves. Absolutely no processed foods. No additives. No preservatives. No artificial colors. No butter. No sugar. What? No sugar?

No kidding! No double-chocolate fudge cream frosting from the can. No Swedish Fish. We're talking raw stuff like crab grass and dandelions—*not* like uncooked cookie dough. No means no, baby. No, no, no!

Only all-natural, *virginal* foods. Pure, *healthy* eats. Will work for food, but this is hard labor!

There are apparently health benefits galore for the macrobiotic devotee, but is this "food for the gods" good for the soul? Suppose it makes you P-M-S cranky?

For someone who was weaned on Twinkies, SpaghettiOs, Dots, and Root Beer Fizzies (don't you just love 'em?), it's an *adjustment* to clean, "healthy" food.

SUGAR. Can't live with it, can't live without it. I love it brown. I love it white. I love it in cubes. I love it as a liquid, gas, and solid. Maple sugar candy is like crack cocaine to this sweet-toothed junkie. My hyperactive pancreas craves it.

Yum. Bulgar wheat and green lentils. Really tasty if you relish a bowlful of sticks and stones. (A little hollandaise sauce would do wonders . . .)

WHEATGRASS. Really, now—should grass be a liquid? And be served in a methadone maintenance cup? Some brave souls down it like vodka shots, but I'll bet Astroturf is tastier.

Need I remind you what happens to your poor dog when he's foolhardy enough to eat grass in the backyard?

The grass is always greener in Fido's food bowl—and she gets kibbles and gravy. Lucky bitch.

SPELT. Never heard of spelt? You're not alone. (But you will be when that stuff kicks in and you're frantic for a restroom.) People who eat spelt *regularly* (don't excuse the pun) are no doubt svelte as a cheese-cutting board. The phrase, "Whoever spelt it, dealt it" will unfortunately come to mind when you load up on this culinary treat.

SEAWEED. Comes in many unappetizing colors, many a shade of gray. Has the texture of shredded cellophane, or maybe extraterrestrial packing material.

(Where's the weed killer and DDT when you really need it?)

With a wheatgrass pickle relish, I can make my own bug spray.

HOW TO MEDITATE

(Transcript from local luminary Willard Pingsley at the Hoboken Holiday Inn)

Ladies, Gentlemen, and Gender Nonidentifying Folks:

I am pleased as spiked punch to be your honored "Be Well, Be Swell" luncheon speaker here at the Malaise and Angst Support Alliance. Hello—or should I say swello?

We in the wellness community were deeply shocked at the untimely demise of your director, Mr. Ervin T. Crabtree III. Goodness, who knew you could overdose on extra-strength canine breath mints?

Life can be a cruel kick below the old belt. Misery caused by a noggin brimming with emotional clutter and toxic memories will make mincemeat of the best egg. And Ervin was a good egg.

On a lighter note, I bring you happiness news from the Department of Awareness and Mindfulness Research Center at Delphic U. Recent studies based more or less on neuroscience indicate that meditation is the magic bullet to ease our body-mind-spirit suffering.

Meditation is a very simple technique. It's not missile surgery; however, keep these critical points in mind as you, um, clear your mind.

Be Positive

Old habits die hard as nails. Your negative thoughts are involved in a conspiracy of cognitive mischief to make you sick as a doggone cougar on a hot tin roof.

Has the bank foreclosed on your home? Wife skipped out on you? Kids delete your texts? Slap a smiley on your har-har-heartbreak.

Pardon me . . . I promised myself I wouldn't cry.

Meditation is Serious Business

No matter how foolish you feel, there's seriously *no* giggling, *no* chuckling, *no* snorting, and especially *no* guffawing in meditation.

Be Kind to Yourself

Relax your body. Loosen that rigid grip that makes you want to choke your spouse. Focus on the muscles you're clenching . . . and release. Stop that squeezing!

You Must Remember to Breathe

When I'm despondent, I forget to breathe, and I turn a peculiar shade of cyan. This makes me unduly twitchy and ruins many an intimate moment.

Take a deep breath. Hold it . . . let it out. Oops, there goes someone's toupee.

Trust

In order to meditate effectively, you must trust not only the loving universe, but also yourself. Close your eyes. No peeking.

Affirmations

Affirmations are the meat of the nut. Repeat after me:

I am humble.

I am happy.

I am mellow . . . or should I say swellow?

Please note that meditation is more effective if you *put the cheesecake and decaf down.*

Let us continue . . . close both eyes.

I am calm.

I am patient.

I am peaceful. Oops, someone fainted at the front table. Remember to *breathe!*

After me:

I am well.

I am wonderful.

I am woman. Hear me roar. I feel pretty, oh so pretty. Sorry, too many good vibrations.

In conclusion: swaddle your soul in meditative bliss, and soon you'll find yourself in fine fettle, hale and hearty, bursting with frivolity, and . . . well, just swell.

Namaste . . .

Whatever that means.

AFFIRMATIONS FOR THE PAINED

- I honor the bitter lemon tree.

- Dark clouds piss on my pretty suede party shoes.

- What goes around comes around . . . and pokes me in the eye.

- The dog doesn't think much of me. I languish in his disappointment.

- It's the little things that bring me such misery.

- Tomfoolery doesn't strike my fancy.

INTRODUCING...
THE 1040-F.I.* FORM
*THE TAX RETURN FOR THE FINANCIALLY INCOMPETENT

① How much money do you guess you made last year?
- ☐ Under $10,000.
- ☐ Somewhere between $10,000 and $100,000.
- ☐ More than $100,000, but I don't know how or why.

② Did you save any receipts?
- ☐ I tried, but I just couldn't.
- ☐ I think there're some in a shoebox. I'll go look.
- ☐ No. What am I, an <u>accountant</u>?

③ Check payment preference.
- ☐ How could I owe anything? My year was lousy.
- ☐ Here's $15,000. If you need more, let me know.
- ☐ Blank check enclosed. <u>You</u> fill it in. Whatever.

APRIL

FISCAL FOLLY

"Money can't buy happiness, but it does bring you
a more pleasant form of misery."

—SPIKE MULLIGAN

TAXES

Time to empty your vacation savings and extinguish those luxury beach resort fantasies. It's (drumroll) tax time.

YOU OWE TOO MUCH

Not a cure-all for your financial woes, but perhaps bankruptcy is an option? Consider filing Chapter 7 or 11. Look at it as a Band-Aid for the hemorrhaging. Yes, it'll hurt like hell to put it on *and* pull it off. Actually, it might just stick forever.

If you're the clever, creative type, perhaps you can fake your death and drop off the face of the earth for a decade or two. Yachts and tropical islands are usually key in this nefarious scenario. Not for the faint of heart or anyone who likes to post on Facebook or go to the dentist regularly.

MONEY: YOU DON'T HAVE ENOUGH

Don't feel bad. Apparently even billionaires and zillionaires feel like they don't have enough. Deep inside, it seems that most people are grossly insecure and dirt poor. Except Buddhists like the Dalai Lama and Richard Gere. Affirmations such as "I am rich" and "I deserve to be rolling in it" often help ease the pain . . . temporarily.

CASH FLOW

When you think of flow, what do you think of? (Besides that.) The flow is light. The flow is heavy. It's *on*. It's *off*. It's more or less regular. In order to have a steady stream of cash to live high on the hog, you must budget and save. The word *budget* comes from Pig Latin and means "stop spending money on fun stuff."

Experts tell you to pay yourself first. They lie. Trust me—you need to pay the IRS first. Then you pay the mortgage company. Then the electricity company. Then the water company. Like your garbage picked up? Then the refuse company. It goes on and on and on to infinity.

11 MONEY TIPS

The economy sucks big time. Therefore, we must cut corners. We must stuff our piggy banks 'til they burst at the seams. We must pinch pennies 'til they scream to be tossed into the nearest fountain.

Here are 11 Money-Saving TIPS . . . you may not have seen elsewhere!

1. Recycling dental floss requires some imagination (and admittedly it's fairly gross), but if you're conscientious about oral hygiene (and I hope you are), you'll rake in the bucks.

2. The kitchen whisk doubles nicely as a head massager. Self-pleasure is the name of the game here. The moola spent on masseuse fees and the hours spent begging your spouse for a freebie are gone—voila!

3. Who needs Meatless Mondays? Why not Meatless Months and Supper-Free Seasons for bona fide fiscal impact?

4. Join the legions of losers who subscribe religiously to Waffle Week. Frozen waffles

make a dandy meal for the entire family. And they're only $3.59 a box ($3.49 if you have a lousy coupon).

5. Let's see how much they really love you! Shake down Gramps and Granny for some serious dental gold, old cigarette lighters, brass knuckles, and silver fountain pens. While you're at it, filch the sterling tea service in the dining room they never use. Then beat a beeline with your shiny stash to the local pawnbroker or gold dealer for some quick cash.

6. The pet toy business is a $25 billion industry; however, you need not spend big dollars to keep your pets feeling adored and entertained. A goldfish cracker on kite string or used dental floss (see Tip #1) makes a nifty cat toy for Little Fluffy (and she'll thank you for the fresher breath).

7. Skippy loves to play, too. According to humorist Dawn Weber, asphalt makes a fine (and free) dog chew toy. After dark, take the kids and head over to the nearby interstate with your handy jackhammer. Drill, baby, drill. Bag yourself some choice chunks. Hours of pleasure for puppy.

8. Instead of purchasing a custom-made birthday cake from a high-end bakery for those special family members, how about a vat of communal hummus and day-old cupcakes? Yum.

9. I realize this is a touchy subject, but please consider diluting your daily bottles of Mom Wine. This will make it stretch a little longer, thus saving you a load of loot (and perhaps a few brain cells, too). Don't worry, be happy!

10. Home energy costs got you down? Turn the heater off. For warmth, fetch those old, sad holiday candles you've been hoarding and light up. Tell your children you're conducting an at-home study unit on colonial America. Wow, how our spunky settlers dealt with *their* bitter cold winters!

11. Vacations are so passé. Staycations are the thing now. What an excellent opportunity to camp out on your sofa, binge on Costco snacks, and catch up on juicy episodes of *The Real Housewives of Beverly Hills* and *The Real Housewives of New Jersey*. Watching those crazy broads roll in the dough is, at least, a vicarious kick. FACTOID: Donna Reed invented the staycation in the classic film *It's a Wonderful Life*. "No money for that honeymoon in Hawaii? No problem! We got chickens on the spit!" Right in our living room! Hooray!

COME FLY WITH ME!

Humorist Robert Benchley voiced his opinion on travel beautifully: "In America, there are two classes of travel: first class, and with children."

Many miss the glory days of early air travel, when flying was downright sexy and adventurous. Even glamorous! People wore their Sunday best and treated the occasion as if it were important.

Today, there are two classes of air travel: private jet and commercial. To most of us, commercial, of course, means coach. Coach is not to be confused with the company that creates stylish designer leather goods. That would suggest a level of quality not experienced with commercial travel.

Flying coach has become ever so unpleasant. Forget dubious TSA gropings and medical-grade X-rays. Forget exorbitant surcharges, inflated fees, and paying for stale peanuts. Forget cramped seats with precious little wiggle room. That's all pretty much expected.

It's the assault on one's senses that irks us. The majority of passengers are scruffy, smelly, and in sore need of an etiquette manual. Need I remind you passengers have urinated in the aisles and made inappropriate deposits on the food carts? Are *we* uncomfortable yet? Ah, oui!

On a recent cross-country trip, I endured what felt like the sleepover from hell with 115 unkempt strangers. All of them treated the cabin as if it were their private dorm room. It was *Animal House* on wings, barreling through the sky at 1,500 mph.

Unfortunately, these are often peeps you wouldn't converse with in a stuck elevator.

The waitresses—sorry, I mean flight attendants—were downright grouchy, and understandably so, considering they obviously don't sleep like normal people. They have what I call "jet nag." I've had it since 1995. There's no cure.

My attendant (Big Marge) barked at passengers as she hawked reeking egg and sausage sandwiches and resentfully swiped Visa cards. It was like being at Denny's, but with higher prices, fewer selections, bad coffee, and no bacon.

After an endless parade of filthy T-shirts, snarly tattoos, and flip-flops, I spotted an urbane, nattily dressed fellow strolling down the aisle. Crisp French blue shirt, pressed tie with gold clasp, sharp crease in his suit pants. Hallelujah! A passenger? No, it was the lovely flight attendant from First Class. God bless his buffed Bruno Magli loafers.

AFFIRMATIONS FOR THE MONEY MISERABLE

- Death and taxes taunt me every day.
- Joy avoids me . . . as do winning lottery numbers.
- I pray for abundance in the form of an electronic bank error.
- I daily feel the lightness in my 401K.
- I live to shop with other people's money.
- Love can't buy me money.

MAY

SICK & TIRED

> "The misery of man proceeds not from any single crush of overwhelming evil, but from small vexations continually repeated."
>
> —SAMUEL JOHNSON

DEATH BY A THOUSAND PAPER CUTS

"To live is to suffer. Find some meaning to your suffering." Sure, Friedrich Nietzsche. Easy for you to say! You're dead.

How do we cope with anxiety, addiction, and existential dread?

I maintain that being miserable is a strategy. First and foremost, it's important to understand and appreciate *the process*.

THE FOUR STAGES OF MISERY

1. WORRY needlessly about all the unlikely yet possible calamities that may befall you. This is, of course, a futile exercise in negative goal setting. Knock yourself out!

2. RELISH your misery as it plays out. Pain sure is an attention-getting kick in the keister.

3. COMMUNICATE your misery to the entire world. Share away—especially on social media and TV. Bask in the vast media markets available to professional victims; consider a reality show or a YouTube channel. Keep in mind: there is *no* such thing as TMI. *We* feel your pain.

4. REMEMBER the anguish and all the mindless minutiae associated with it. Never forget. PTSD is the gift that keeps coming . . . and coming . . . and coming. We are *all* gifted in this ability to torture ourselves.

ILLNESS

At any given time in your life, you will be sick as a dog. And even when you're not officially ill, you may exhibit symptoms of several debilitating ailments simultaneously. It may be all in your head, but more likely it's a result of what's in your head. Years of worries and woe are festering in your brain and metastasizing to your vital organs—

especially your heart.

You're sick. You're tired. As a matter of fact, you're sick *and* tired.

My prescription? Give yourself a break. You need a mental health day, not only from work, but from your exhausting life. If a day isn't sufficient, feel free to take a week or a month. A year off—although tempting—will most likely be too much of a good thing (unless you live in Portland).

SLEEP—THE HARD FACTS

If you're female, you don't get enough sleep. This is because women are generally thoughtful and caring individuals. This quirk will keep you awake at 3:00 a.m. like a screeching car alarm.

It seems that sleep is elusive to those who have a functioning brain. Also, fluctuating hormones can be a contributing factor to insomnia. As a psychiatrist told me, "You're particularly susceptible to sleep disorders if you don't drink enough." Hmmm. Bottoms up!

Lack of sleep is connected to cognitive deterioration, foul moods, poor makeup application, and eventual complete disintegration.

Sleep, like sex and chocolate, is essential for survival.

Daydreaming, zoning out, and naps are all good for you. Indulge as often as possible.

Outsource your worrying.

Also important to remember: Sleep is "Peels" backwards. Don't slip on it.

CONFESSION

Tsk, tsk. The sordid rumors you've heard about me are, alas, sadly true. The scoop on the street does not obfuscate. I confess: I can't get enough. I can never get enough. Actually, I can't get any. Sleep, that is.

I crave it like a duck craves H20, like a fruit fly hankers after a steaming hot mound of apple cinnamon oatmeal, like Lady Gaga lusts for a crazy heinie new hat.

Ever since I hit forty with all the calm of a head-on collision, my circadian clock has a cuckoo bird diddling royally with the rhythms, the REM cycle, the NREM spin cycle, the wash and rinse, the eternally stuck snooze alarm.

I grapple in the black hole of terminal crabbiness, cognitive dysfunction, and impaired moral judgment, not to mention severe, really annoying yawning. Hard to believe, but my grooming and hygiene no doubt suffer, too.

How I envy the young hottie whose beauty sleep comes as easily as the flick and flutter of her long, full eyelashes. Bah hum ladybug to you, Missy!

I've indulged in all the usual tired remedies for my malady: asinine herbal bedtime snacks, lavender inhalants, listening to opera, reading physics journals, watching C-SPAN, even, dear God, conversing with chatty in-laws.

In my pathetic struggle to grasp the ever-elusive somnolent high, that sweet, soothing rush of warm melatonin oozing into the nooks and crannies of my weary perimenopausal brain, I have sunk to limbo-level lows. I've become a valerian junkie, an Advil PM addict, a NoDoz abuser. I'll do anything, perhaps everything, for some measly Z's. I'd kill to sleep like a log. I'd pay a million bucks for forty winks.

And so it is with blubbering shame and significant personal disgust that I—in the still of my bleakest, starless nights—dip into my private cache of smut for the sleep deprived. The images I've secreted away on my computer: bright pictures of chirpy, well-rested couples in TempurPedic ads; cheerful fellows napping in comfy backyard hammocks; tanned women dozing blissfully on massage tables at Maui resorts; and, worst of all, seductive color spreads of that narcoleptic Disney slacker Sleeping Beauty.

Cruelly, even my computer sleeps, and I succumb to dire fantasies of being hooked up to a Propofol intravenous cocktail, consciousness suspended, postural muscles relaxed in a nerve-numbing fog. How I long to be in the land of Nod, yearn to be limp in the arms of Morpheus. Oy, where art thou, sweet slumber? Rolling like thunder under the covers? Bosh! Sleep—it's the new sex.

WHAT KEEPS YOU UP AT NIGHT?

25 Reasons I Can't Sleep!

1. The industrial-strength garlic in the pasta carbonara I had for lunch.

2. The dog is snoring like a moose and drooling on my pillow.

3. Can't turn off my brain.

4. I'm hot.

5. I'm cold.

6. I need sex so badly my cavities ache.

7. *Memory... all alone in the moonlight... I can smile at the old days.* What Broadway musical was that darn song from ... and why am I craving salmon?

8. I have Restless LEGO Syndrome (my inner child *still* can't fit all the pieces together).

9. I'm hungry.

10. I ate too much marbleized meat at dinner.

11. I saw that damn movie *Snakes on a Plane*.

12. Was there infected cantaloupe in that overpriced fruit salad I had yesterday? OMG, do I have listeria?

13. I'm not the least bit superstitious—but there will be *no* #13.

14. My Visa bill is due in two weeks.

15. Justin Bieber

16. Male menopause

17. Knowing the Kardashians are laughing all the way to the bank

18. My young boyfriend

19. My young girlfriend

20. Your husband (The restraining order isn't working.)

21. I drank a pot of espresso after 5:00 p.m. and now I can't close my eyes. I may have to duct tape them shut.

22. The national debt

23. All politicians

24. There's one more slice of chocolate birthday cake left in the fridge, and it's got my name on it.

25. Space junk is gonna fall on my face any day; I just know it.

WHY YOU SHOULD NEVER TAKE HAPPINESS ADVICE FROM A LAWYER

What do they know? Lawyers, as a group, are a fairly miserable bunch. They're historically (often rightly so) maligned and despised. They often have the good taste to abhor themselves.

MEDIC ALERT BRACELETS FOR PEOPLE WE HATE

We have medical alert bracelets for chronic medical conditions, drug allergies, and medications we're taking.

According to the Medic Alert Foundation's "Who Should Wear a Medical ID?" criteria it's anyone with Alzheimer's, diabetes, food allergies, heart disease, asthma, COPD, penicillin allergies, epilepsy.

But . . .

How about alert bracelets for the people we really need to be aware of?

For instance, these lovely folks:

- **Flake:** La, la, la. Whichever way the wind is blowing is where you'll find me. Maybe that's 'cause I'm an airhead. So what if you can't count on me to commit to anything I couldn't stick to a plan if you dipped me in Krazy Glue. Whatever.

- **Liar:** Lying is in my DNA. I will astound you with the ease with which I lie like hell. I'm smooth as a baby's behind. No wonder I'm a lawyer, and I'm probably running for president too; my skills are perfectly suited to politics.

- **Phony:** I'm superficial and hollow to the core. I sincerely don't give a whit about you, but I get a buzz from pretending I care. It's my inside joke on all the suckers who cross my path, and it amuses me to no end. You guessed it—Hollywood is dear to my heart.

- **Bore:** Attempt to have a conversation with me, and pretty soon you'll see it's all about *me, me, me.* True, most consider me a pompous ass and a blowhard, but they're just jealous! As an important person, I have a duty to pontificate 'til you succumb to my power.

- **Cheapskate:** Beware when dining or traveling with me! I'll order a bottle of vintage wine, seafood appetizers, the most expensive meat entrée on the menu, dessert, cappuccino, and cognac—then split the bill fifty-fifty with you. So what if you're on a five-day cleanse and only had chicken broth? BTW, I seem to have a bit of a memory problem, as I frequently "forget" my wallet.

- **Drama Queen:** OMG! The sky is falling! The sky is falling! I barely have enough energy left to snap this crappy alert bracelet on my feeble wrist.

- **Snob:** My nose is so far up in the air I've got a permanent case of whiplash. You're so far beneath me I need an electron microscope to see you. What? How dare you speak to me. Go away, peasant!

- **Bitch:** I'll stab you in the back—and sometimes in the front—if I damn well feel like it. Be my frenemy at your own risk.

As you can see, this product can save a lot of anguish and time spent on doomed friendships and ill-advised marriages. Consider it preventive care for the psyche. It's cheaper than counseling and couples' therapy! Maybe we can get your crackerjack health insurance company to cover it. (Don't hold your breath.)

Medic Alert bracelets for people we hate—coming to a pharmacy or drive-thru Starbucks near you! Also available, alert bracelets for the Schmuck, Hypocrite, Bully, Wimp, Cheater, Mama's Boy, and Princess.

AFFIRMATIONS FOR THE SICK AND TIRED

- My joints ache with every new sunrise.

- Every cell in my body vibrates with despair.

- Embarrassing nail fungus has infinite power over me.

- Social interaction drains me like a heavy menstrual period.

- A good night's sleep eludes me.

- My eyeballs embrace all the beauty in the world, as well as the pathogenic bacteria.

"If the hat persists, call me."

JUNE

LONELINESS

> "Friends love misery, in fact. Sometimes, especially if we are too lucky or too successful or too pretty, our misery is the only thing that endears us to our friends."
>
> —ERICA JONG

Are you singing the blues? Feeling as lonely as a classic country song? Hurtin' like a haunting Amy Winehouse, Edith Piaf, or Billie Holiday ballad? Honey, you're crooning to the boohoo chorus.

JUNE GLOOM

In the United States, as in most of the sad world, you have weather. You have a variety of weather patterns and temperature changes, as well as four seasons. This isn't the case in coastal Southern California. As you know, we're *special*.

In Los Angeles, we have consistently perfect weather—sunny with temperatures in the seventies. It's a truly reasonable climate that only the most miserable among us (usually transplanted New Yorkers) find unacceptable. These are the cranks who complain about unending sunshine and clear skies as if it's a *bad* thing. "I miss the seasons," they whine.

However, even for the easy to please, there is an ugly shoofly in *The Endless Summer of SoCal* . . . and that is the infamous "June Gloom."

According to Wikipedia (who else?), June Gloom is "a weather pattern that results in cloudy, overcast skies with cool temperatures during the late spring and early summer, most commonly in the month of June." (This is why it's not called February Gloom.)

"Low-altitude stratus clouds are formed over the ocean, then transported over the coastal regions by the wind."

Translation: June Gloom is a month-long period of fog and drizzle up the yahoo where you feel like an abuse victim in a never-ending Bergman movie. I call it *50 Shades of L.A. Gray*.

June Gloom should be a bona fide mental disorder ordained by the American Psychiatric Association. It's Los Angeles's version of seasonal affective disorder.

We all know that long, snowy winters with subzero temperatures are depressing. But, after all, that's what you ordered if you live in Butte, Montana, or Caribou, Maine. Not La-La Land!

It's all about expectations. In Southern California coastal regions (aka the beach), we expect to see and feel the *sun*—duh! After all, we don't go to the beach for the rain.

It's disconcerting to gaze out your window in Malibu and see nothing but gray clouds and white fog. Geez! Is it snowing? You can kiss that million-dollar view goodbye for a month or two. June has no mercy.

True—snow, sleet, and hail are direct assaults on the mood, but they're for sissies.

Fog and drizzle are insidious . . . the guerrilla warfare of weather. They hang over your head like an ominous dark cloud and tease you with a feeble ray of sunlight every hour or so. This generates false, painful hope in the hapless optimist. As many know too well, "Hollywood will kill you with its optimism."

June Gloom is the original *Summer Bummer*.

PUPPY LOVE

The other day, my good friend Carla (no doubt delirious on endorphins from our morning walk with our dogs) shared this juicy nibble with me: "I'd like to marry Clifford. He's the perfect companion." She air-kissed Clifford, her aging basset hound (names have been changed to protect *me*).

Acquainted with the less-than-captivating personality of Bob, her husband of fifteen years, I saw her point; however, I'm not dumb enough to kick her crotchety husband while he's in the doghouse, so I faked amusement: "Oh, really? You're such a kidder."

Carla felt compelled to elaborate on her infatuation with her four-legged bud: "Clifford, in spite of his sloppy eating habits, nonexistent table manners, and horrible breath, is quite the mellow fellow, an easygoing little guy." She bent over and kissed him on the lips.

I laughed. "Too bad his ears sweep the floor and his brain is smaller than his anus." Carla looked miffed, so I offered her a bone. "Clifford is very sweet. You enrich each other's lives. That's what counts."

She gushed, "He's always in a good mood."

Forget about *marrying* your dog. Wouldn't it be nice to *be* your dog?

Your dog is happy. He's a success. His family loves him. He loves his family.

He appreciates simple pleasures like the wind in his face, the joy of a w-a-l-k, the thrill of a tummy rub, the pride of peeing on a worm, the indulgence of a long nap on the sofa, the treat of raw hamburger, the delight of a "sniff and kiss" with a curvaceous redhead—even if she is a golden retriever.

Life as your dog . . . it doesn't get any better than that.

DAILY STRATEGIES FOR OPTIMIZING YOUR MISERY

You'll find the following tips so helpful that you'll send me your life savings via electronic bank transfer.

1. Watch early-morning TV shows.

2. Immerse yourself in anything remotely political.

3. Sit at a desk for hours on end.

4. Attempt to bathe the dog, or worse yet, dogs.

5. Engage in small talk with small people.

6. Deprive yourself of chocolate before noon.

7. Answer phone calls willy-nilly instead of ignoring them.

8. Ask people how they *really* feel.

9. Avoid your favorite indulgences (see #6).

10. Have daily histrionic sulking fits like a five-year-old.

11. Carp, bark, and nag your spouse just because you can.

12. Keep your frenemies close to your heart.

13. Go broke spending big bucks on a personal trainer and life coach.

14. Make play and silliness a task on your "Work" list.

15. Quote Chesterton and Michel de Montaigne incessantly.

16. Read too many happiness books.

CLUTTER KILLS

Do your belongings weigh you down? Is your closet brimming with clothes you don't wear? Is your garage full of junk? Do the responsibility, hassle, and expense of ownership make you feel as overwhelmed as a tonsil with strep?

The Minimalist Movement is a lifestyle trend based on the philosophy that having fewer material items will make you happier. Simplicity and peace of mind are achieved by intentionally minimalist living.

I suspect unemployed and underemployed Millennials who can't afford to buy lots of cool stuff started this movement. After all, not everybody aspires to live in a tiny house the size of a roach motel.

But perhaps a smaller home, no car, and fewer possessions would make *you* happier?

Fine. I'll take that Lexus coupe and Chanel jacket off your hands!

Is that ski chalet in Aspen a painful burden to you?

No problem. I'll take care of it for you.
Dying to unload that cumbersome Gulfstream G650?
If you insist. Sign it over. That's what friends are for.
Remember! *Clutter, especially in the cardiac arteries, can kill.*

HAIL THE BLESSED ONE!

At that time the Buddha, the Blessed One, was dwelling at Uruvelā at the foot of the Bo-tree on the banks of the river Nerañjarā, having just attained the Buddhaship. The Blessed One sat cross-legged for seven days together at the foot of the Bo-tree experiencing the bliss of emancipation.
—Translated from *The Mahā-Vagga*
(Harvard Classics, 1909–14)

Hail the Blessed One!

No, not Buddha, but my priority-challenged husband of twenty-odd years, who has been gifted with the luxury of seven days at home alone with the TV remote, the absurdly easygoing dog (a real sap), the pragmatic cat, an uncharacteristically light work schedule, and a grease-stained take out menu from Pizza Express—hold the mushrooms, extra-thick crust, and heavy on the peppers, please.

Ohm. While the Blessed One experiences the bliss of emancipation, his menopausal wife and hormonally turbocharged teenage daughter journey three thousand miles away to a pastoral college campus in quaint New England (or is it Canada?). Our mission: to move the budding scholar into her living space (*dorm* is so pedestrian) for the school year. It's an annual parent-child rite of passage, a sacred feat of family organization complete with lavender-scented drawer paper and elaborate photo collage memo boards.

Ohm. Ohm. The Blessed One sits in serene navel contemplation as we gals trudge through three pandemic-infected airports, are no doubt stalked by terrorists at every turn, suffer crippling body cramps (can you say "sciatica"?) from the circulation-crushing coach seats, are jarred by brain-rattling rental car shuttle buses, battle a violent downpour on the interstate, and are rudely insulted by rest stop bathrooms with no toilet paper.

Ohm. Ohm. Ohm. We schlep across three time zones carting a year's worth of Young Missy clothing for all seasons (gosh, denim is heavy), winter shoes and boots (can you say *Uggh*), the mandatory collection of fashion accessories, a computer, a color printer, enough electronic paraphernalia for a professional gamer, and a heavy guitar with an even heavier guitar case.

Back at the ranch, the Blessed One is engrossed in the spiritual realm—not under the Mucalinda tree but on a comfy velveteen sofa in front of a big-screen TV.

Then the Blessed One,
concerning this, on that occasion,
breathed forth this solemn utterance:
"How blest the happy solitude
Of him who hears and knows the truth!

*How blest is harmlessness toward all,
And self-restraint toward living things!"*

How blest the happy solitude indeed. Upon my harried return, seven physically draining, excruciatingly melodramatic, hot-flashing, liver-wrenching days later, it was clear my husband's brain had taken a mini spa vacation while I was away.

To his credit, he arrives at the airport more or less on time, but not, of course, in time to park. It's the familiar drive-by pickup long-married spouses know so well. ("Quick, jump in before we get a ticket!")

Curiously, he's wearing a hat, something he rarely does. But it's not just any hat. It's a *new* hat.

The hat is an expensive, imported item from Scotland with a precious royal name and a tiny red feather in its silk ribbon band. It appears to be several sizes too large (the word *pinhead* comes to mind, but I bite my lip.) It's flamboyant in a way only my gay guy friends could love, and, tragically, paid for online with a debit card. I learn that it was express mailed two days before in grand style, obviously traveling more lavishly than I have in the past week.

"I missed you, honey," offers the Blessed One (nice try).

It seems the tank hasn't been filled, so we have the pleasure of gassing up next to a gang-infested taco joint perilously close to the tarmac. "Oops, forgot," shrugs the One.

"Dinner will be nice after a day of stale granola bars, Bcano, and airline coffee," I say hopefully.

"Oh, like a regular meal?" he says perplexedly. And so to prolong the endless day of travel yet another hour, we stop at a grocery store on the way home, as the idea of replenishing basic food staples hasn't crossed his spiritually enlightened mind. (Did he forget the dog also eats? In fact, he lives to eat. Did he forget we have a cat?)

As we enter the house, the One casually mentions he's noticed a mysterious smell at the top of the stairs for several days. I smell nothing because I'm numb with jet lag and my sinuses are as swollen as softballs. (I wonder if that happens in first class.)

The dog greets me like a long-lost lover. Gleeful as a drunken sailor, he jumps frantically to and fro, throwing kisses and running amuck "au naturel"—no collar, no leash, and no tags. (The party's over, Buster; we got laws—the sheriff's back in town!)

Also waiting to greet me is an overflowing wastebasket, a landfill of dirty laundry, two popped light bulbs, a rearranged kitchen with no evidence of cooking whatsoever, a plastic plant that has been generously watered, and window blinds askew in every room. (How *can* he sleep at night?)

The DVR recordings tell the dirty tale. My priceless episodes of *What Not to Wear* and *Martha Stewart* brutally deleted in favor of tedious third-world soccer matches and National Geographic documentaries on glowworm lint.

As my sinuses crack open ever so painfully, a homicidal stench punches me squarely in the face. (This can't be good. I envision hazmat teams breaking the doors down any minute.)

A neighbor calls to inform me that the cat has been staying at her house for the week. She's enjoyed the company, but the tuna bill is adding up.

Nauseated by the sheer toxicity of "the smell," I stumble upstairs in search of the source. "I don't think the dog peed on the carpet," the Blessed One opines. Gagging, I brace myself, scour the bedrooms, then peek in the guest bathroom. The window is wide open, the lock disengaged, and the security stick is on the floor. "Gee, I wonder where that stink is coming from?" Buddha inquires of the universe. Suffice it to say, the source of "the smell" turned out to be a rather obvious lapse in basic bathroom plumbing etiquette.

How blest from passion to be free,
All sensuous joys to leave behind!
Yet far the highest bliss of all
To quit th' illusion false—I am.

They can make a miracle blue tablet for an eighty-five-year-old to have an erection for five hours, four of which he's probably napping, but not for a fifty-year-old dude to remember to feed the dog, empty the trash, and flush the toilet.

Ohm. Hail the Blessed One.

AFFIRMATIONS FOR THE LONELY

- I coddle my inner curmudgeon.
- I am allergic to feel-good endorphins.
- I will never be pretty, oh so pretty.
- Life is one colossal mind suck.
- Mother Nature and Father Time are abusive to me.
- The mysterious appeal of pimento cheese will confound me 'til my dying day.

JULY

POOP CULTURE

"Misery is a communicable disease."
—MARTHA GRAHAM

I FEEL YOUR PAIN

I feel your pain. Do you feel mine? I bet you do. Yes, I refer to that niggling, noggin-splitting pain, that bone-gnawing anguish, that teeming existential angst we experience whenever we face the Ugly Truth.

You know what I'm talking about, for like my humble self, you too are a highly discerning individual: intellectually aware, artistically appreciative, cultivated, indubitably enlightened to a T.

We are kindred souls, you and I, we folks of gentle nature. We cringe at double negatives and dangling participles as if they were sidewalk spit or public urination (they might as well be, you say!). We're dumbstruck by blatant ignorance as if it were a whack to the side of the skull with a cricket bat. We recoil when garish tattoos and vile body piercings mar the landscape like graffiti violates a beautiful city's grand architecture. (May I suggest a stiff gimlet, heavy on the Rose's?)

The Ugly Truth cuts like a meat cleaver. Civilization, such as it is, faces extinction due to the man-made Global Deformation of Culture. Dial 911 pronto, fellow citizens!

This pop culture pollution isn't limited to innocuous pockets of urban-dwelling deviants, multimillionaire shock jocks, slum landlords, porn stars, scum lawyers (excuse the redundancy), horny politicians, the prison populace, Hollywood wannabes, network TV executives, and New Jersey housewives. No sirree! That humongous slick of putrid multimedia excrement flowing to our pristine daisy-adorned doorsteps has transmogrified entire gaggles of society. An invasion of our finer senses and inherent good taste is imminent. Fortify yourself, friends! (It would be prudent to stock up on alcohol.) Great art—classical music, literature, painting, philosophy, haiku, for heaven's sake—is under threat. Nothing is sacrosanct.

Hear the torturous drip, drip, drip? Plop, plop, plop? I share your despair. Numbed down to drooling Neanderthals, we'll likely drown in an incessant data deluge of toxic D-list celebrity drivel, insidious social sell, and narcissistic blah, blah, blah. Pray tell, wouldn't it be lovely if technology elevated culture instead of infecting it like an STD?

What we have now is Culture with a *K*. Good grief, the krappy (pardon my French) Kardashians make poor Paris Hilton look like Grace Kelly. The hussies carp, kvetch, and curse 'til the cash cows come home to their leopard-print Beverly Hills mansions, tacky Tribeca penthouses, and gauche South Beach luxury condos. How I ache for a culture that ennobles the soul.

The pain, the pain—will it ever end? Compadres, unite! Uncork that precious bottle of Château Lafite Rothschild Bordeaux '85 you've been saving for just such a crisis, put your sorry feet up on a plump ottoman, and immerse yourself in Shakespeare, Mozart, Flaubert, Schumann. I'll set society's GPS for civility, refinement, and urbanity. I fear they are, alas, lost somewhere over the rainbow in cyberspace.

CELEBRITY STUPID

There's way too much nepotism and inbreeding in show biz, in the funeral industry, and in politics. It's not only who you know—it's who knows you.

Shouldn't *celebrity* be spelled sell*ebrity*?

> *In Buddhism, the purpose of life is to end suffering.*
> *The Buddha taught that humans suffer because*
> *we continually strive after things that do not give*
> *us lasting happiness.*
>
> —*A Pictorial History of Medicine*
> by Otto L. Mettmann

If you want to end suffering, you can always turn off the TV and the computer.

REALITY TV: GARBAGE IN, GARBAGE OUT

For many of us, watching reality TV is a serious hobby that consumes a large portion of our leisure (if not waking) time. We accept that many unenlightened souls prefer reading poetry, going to the opera, playing golf or canasta, attending lectures at museums, serving the community, or collecting antique gnomes. Tsk. Tsk.

In reality TV (especially the *Real Housewives* variety), we have drama with a capital B. We have all seven deadly sins represented, plus a few extra ones wrapped in a decadent Twinkie for the soul.

Voyeurism is a form of envy. We envy the glamorous, exciting, celebrity-sucked lives of the truly disturbed in New York City and Beverly Hills. Thanks to the internet, cable TV, tabloid journalism, and cell phone cameras, we have a twenty-four-seven backstage pass to the Fab Freak Fest.

When there are no rules, there are no sins. The fascination with reality TV is that the "characters" live in a morality-free zone. Anything goes. Shacking up with your friend's boyfriend, having sex with the kitchen help, flaunting hookups with the pubescent interns, or diddling your dry cleaner is perfectly cool in this fantasyland.

Perhaps there should be a warning label on these shows: More than five hours' viewing can cause toxic schlock syndrome, a condition known to kill brain cells.

The philosophical questions remain: Does art imitate life, or does life imitate art? Does reality TV reflect life, or does life reflect reality TV? If Edvard Munch's painting *The Scream* is alone in the forest, does it make a sound? What's sexier, boxers or briefs?

If you add the f word to art, do you get *fart*?

BOOB TUBE

Condolences are in order: my only TV died the other day. On Friday at 7:23 p.m. smack in the middle of an acid reflux commercial, to be exact. True, it was getting on in years, and yes, there had been a prolonged illness with much suffering, mostly mine. In my mourning, I flirted with the notion of never replacing that boob tube and instead reading the world's greatest books again (okay, for the first time), this time in Latin.

I quickly came to my senses. With cranky college kids coming home for lengthy breaks, it seemed clear as a school bell that family harmony (read: survival) was dependent on having a working TV.

And so in the spirit of consumerism and a fierce dedication to eternal debt, my husband and I decided to thumb our noses at the global recession, the impending economic implosion, and stormy weather.

Instead of investing in gold bricks and food insurance or maxing out the ol' credit cards to feed the feral kitties, clothe the whales, or educate the cockatoos, we decided to buy a big-screen TV. Now we can watch the collapse of Western civilization in the relative comfort of our cozy, vacuum-challenged living room. Yippee!

This purchase necessitated venturing forth to the Big Idiot Box Store, on a work night, no less. Armed with a handful of dubious online coupons, we descend into the discount dungeon via steep one-way escalators. This is retail hell: five hundred giant TVs jacked up to a "fright bright" setting, all blaring obscenely. This doesn't prime me for a buying frenzy. Rather it screams "the mother of all bloody migraines!"

The choices confound. Widescreen, theater vision, stadium size, ultra HD, LCD, LED, plasma, 3D. How much "p" and "Hz?" (Do we really want to see that icky skin rash on Ryan Seacrest's neck pop out like an industrial spill?) The sets all display the same exhausting Katy Perry concert video, and they all look . . . the same.

"Size matters. The bigger, the better," the adolescent sales associate insists. (Isn't there a law against child labor? Our cocker spaniel is older than this pup!) After innumerable attempts to upsell us to the Ultra Theater Family Fun Package with PlayStation stereoscopic 3D gaming, the popular game *Grand Turismo Death Call*, the virtual game *Pacific Pain Wipe-Out: Die, Sucka!*, a pair of super cool 3D glasses, high-speed Internet connectivity, and a 3D Blu-ray disc of *Alice in Wonderland*, we settle on a sensible TV—namely the one that's drastically marked down.

Junior pushes it: "Are you sure you don't want that PlayStation? You might regret it." I snort. "Sonny, do we look like we play games?" My husband blurts out, "You don't know what regret is. It's five kids, a shopping cart full of bills, a crippling mortgage, and killer hemorrhoids. On a good night, I collapse in front of the news." "It's true," I chime in. "He's all 'No Nintendo tonight, dear. I'm comatose.'" We laugh heartily as only the truly wise (read: old) can when mocking the blissfully ignorant (read: young).

As Junior cringes in horror, he leads us to the checkout counter and his sales manager "to run the final numbers." My husband groans, "It's easier buying a car."

After a shipload of solicitous prattle from Junior and Beaver, the twenty-year-old sales manager, they swivel a computer screen at us displaying our invoice. "We put you down for protection for three years at $349. If something goes wrong with your set, you don't want to deal with the manufacturer. They really suck."

My husband objects, "We have a warranty, and if the set doesn't work perfectly for the future, we'll bring it back and expect you to personally replace it, with funds from your allowance if necessary. Thank you, no 'protection' for the TV."

Beaver anxiously laughs, then leans in confidingly. "I bought the same set—well actually, a much bigger one—last year, and there was a crazy line up the middle of the screen. I hear that happens a lot, and boy was I glad I ponied up the measly $349 for protection. Just sayin'." What a lying little pipsqueak, I think. Hubby stares at the boy and says, "Do you think we're stupid?" "No!" Beaver insists. "How about this: just for you nice people, I'll give you two years of protection for $299." "No!" my husband and I shout in unison.

I whimper, "My feet are killing me. I need to sit down." My husband throws in the towel too. "I'm going to the men's room." I try to salvage a sliver of civility. I say, "You seem awfully busy. What time do you close? Ten o'clock? Wow, that late!"

Beaver smirks, flips the screen my way, and reels off the extra charges. "It's $59.99 for the deluxe HD cable cord; $129 for the expandable, ultrathin wall mount set; $369 for the two supplemental surround speakers; $69 for delivery, and $199 for calibration by our technician." I bleat, "Calibration? Technician? It's not a jet engine!" Junior scoffs. "Hee, hee. That's cute."

Fifteen minutes later, my husband returns carrying a Tivo Premiere DVR player. (He's gone to the dark side.) "We need one of these so we don't miss anything," he protests weakly.

The blinding auras clutching my eyeballs are ninja migraines poised to sucker punch my brain. I grab my knees, "Gonna vomit . . ."

Beaver drones on, "We can deliver your set two weeks from tomorrow, at the earliest. Delivery will be sometime between 7:00 a.m. and 7:00 p.m. If you want it earlier, there's a surcharge of $99 to move your name up the list. If you want to know what time we're delivering it within a two-hour period, that'll be an additional $79 surcharge."

I wipe my face and gasp. "Oh my God! Don't forget my 15 percent off coupon." He chuckles. "Yes, ma'am. We can apply that to an accessory. Look, I saved you forty-four cents!" Whoopee!

The Beav suddenly hiccups. "Oops. Sorry, folks. I've got to redo this invoice. I must've missed a field or two . . . and gotta add the Tivo." My husband groans. Like a five-year-old I whine, "I'm tired. I wanna go home. My head hurts." Beaver fumbles with the keyboard. "Oops . . ." I grab him by the collar. "Dear God, hurry up, will you?" He presents me with the charge slip. "Geez lady. Here you go." I cover my eyes and sign.

Beaver chirps, "Going out to a nice dinner now, folks?" I snort. "Are you kidding? It's 8:30 p.m." My husband pig piles on. "We're old and we're cranky. We want to go home." Beav smiles. "Oh sure. Then you can open a nice bottle of wine and hang out in your living room." Wink wink.

Four weeks and five technician appointments later, we proudly display our new super duper TV to our visiting teen. He shrugs. "I watch TV on my laptop. It's free. You don't need a TV. Gosh, you guys are so old." Oh well. Too bad I can't find my laptop without a magnifying glass.

By the way, has anyone seen the remote?

FAVORITE FILMS OF MISERABLE PEOPLE*

- *'Night Mother*
- *Caged*
- *Bambi*
- *I Want to Live!*
- *Lés Miserables*
- *Dahmer: The Cannibal*
- *Misery*
- *Das Boot*
- *Million Dollar Baby*
- *Old Yeller*
- *The Killing Fields*
- *Precious*

**Caged* and *Misery* also qualify as two of the funniest films of all time.

FAVORITE SONGS OF MISERABLE PEOPLE

- "Born to Lose" (Ray Charles)
- "Weighty Ghost" (Land of Talk)
- "Being Green" (Kermit)

- "Seasons in the Sun" (Jacques Brel)
- "Hurt" (Johnny Cash)
- "Candle in the Wind" (Elton John)
- "Streets of Philadelphia" (Springsteen)
- "The Sounds of Silence" (Simon & Garfunkel)
- "Back to Black" (Amy Winehouse)
- "Don't Worry Be Happy" (Bobby McFerrin)
- All pop songs in French that feature accordion music, especially ones by Edith Piaf

QUIZ: IS YOUR THINKING MAKING YOU ANXIOUS OR DEPRESSED?

Here's some multiple-choice "edutainment" for you—you who love to reflect and dwell on the crazy stuff in your head. Pick the answer that seems most normal.

1. How would you describe your daily thoughts?

    a. Downright depressing
    b. Irrational and terrifying
    c. Insipid
    d. 100 percent sexual in nature
    e. Realistic and factual

2. Complete this sentiment. "The sun will . . ."

   a. Set in the evening, but I'll miss it 'cause I'll be working late locked in my crappy little cubicle at my low-paying, dead-end job. *Where's Abe Lincoln when you need him?*
   b. Fire gigantic, killer flares that will incinerate Earth and Uranus.
   c. Come up when it damn well feels like it.
   d. Give us all fatal melanomas.
   e. Come out tomorrow. *Betch your bottom dollar.*

3. What are your personal "shoulds" and "musts?"

   a. I should read every self-help book that's out there.
   b. I should exercise every day, or I'll be a big, fat, sickly slob.
   c. I must make more money, or I'm a total loser.
   d. I must, must improve my bust, bust.
   e. I shoulda, coulda, woulda is an unhealthy cliché. Screw that!

4. What are your favorite ways to foolishly fritter away your time and energy?

   a. Worrying, of course
   b. Asinine games on my smarter-than-me phone
   c. Eating junk food while watching trash TV
   d. Working
   e. Spending quality time with my inner child

5. Which of the following are illogical and contradictory beliefs?

    a. Life is a nasty SOB, and then you die.
    b. Life is good; I am bad.
    c. Someone up there has it in for me.
    d. I have horrible luck when it comes to love, the lottery, and Candy Crush.
    e. You can't choose your parents, but you can choose your dog.

Bottom Line: If your thoughts are causing you pain, stop all that stupid thinking! Go out and play.

AFFIRMATIONS FOR THE OVERWHELMED

- I am one with trash TV.

- I marvel at the destructive power unleashed upon me by migraine headaches.

- I feel the warm sun caressing me . . . probably causing me to suffer life-threatening melanomas.

- It is clear I will never have my seven minutes of fame.

- Weather sucks. So do meteorologists who wear clown noses on early morning TV shows.

- My head is full of God knows what.

"I forgot my hair!"

AUGUST

CHAOS

"Life is a constant process of dying."
—ARTHUR SCHOPENHAUER

DRAMA QUEENS UNITE

I'm a drama queen. You most likely are also a drama queen. Your spouse may be one. Your daughter, sister, cousin, and mother are *definitely* drama queens. We won't even mention crazy Aunt Belinda—it's too disturbing for all who come across her.

If only drama queens offered the same sweet refreshment Dairy Queens do—we would welcome them into our dull, controlled lives with open arms.

According to Urban Dictionary, a drama queen is "someone who turns something unimportant into a major deal; someone who blows things way out of proportion whenever the chance is given." *Ding ding!*

We DQs are real Fs—feelers, that is. We make decisions based on our feelings. We're most convinced by how we feel. We take almost everything personally. After all, is there any other way? We wear our hearts on our sleeves, where everybody is free to stomp on them, shit-kick them, and grind them into a fine black-and-blue dust. We love to be complimented, gushed over, and generally sucked up to. This motivates us to draw another breath, face another gray dawn, maybe even survive another day. Violins!

Being a drama queen is a calling. It chooses you. It's like being a doctor, only you're the patient—the mental patient!

It's important to remember that drama isn't something to be confined to Broadway theaters, reality TV, pop song lyrics, and personal episodes of extreme PMS. It's a raison d'être, an identity, a mission.

THE DRAMA QUEEN'S DECLARATION OF DESPAIR

HELP! HELP! HELP!

Hyperbole does not take a holiday.

Overreactions do not take five. There's no break for worry and anxiety, so you may as well revel in it!

Rationality doesn't resonate with DQs, just as emoting doesn't reach a mere thinker. We're talking apples and orangutans.

Happiness is not rocket surgery or quantum physics. *It's a feeling.* Since we drama queens are masters of "the Feeling," we have the power to conjure orgasmic joy or teeth-grinding misery any darn time we please. So there, self-actualized "happiness" cult members! You're amateur twits compared to us. Even though we're occasionally frequently almost always okay, always desolate, we emotional expulsives rule the realm of authenticity. We ain't faking it!

FACTOID: Dentists report that four out of five chirpy, smiley people are big, fat phonies.

SELF-CARE

Quality self-care is essential for strengthening yourself when dealing with life's chaos. The unresolved grief and trauma (real and imagined) from your childhood is no doubt wrecking havoc on your equilibrium, digestion, and liquor budget.

YOUR INNER CHILD

You're simply not practicing self-love when you tell your inner child to go play in traffic.

It's hurtful when you snipe at your inner child, *You're not the sharpest shovel in the sandbox.*

Spend "me time" with your inner me. Neglect is a form of abuse. You don't want to have to post this on Twitter: *My inner child ran away from home. #missing*

Your inner tyke may be wearing a tiara and jester cap, but chances are she/he is singing "It's My Party and I'll Cry if I Want To."

Yes, your inner child is crying. Your job as an adult is to comfort your inner little person. Give your inner child a break (not literally). Be kind and loving—you know, as if you were talking to your dog.

After all, your mind is a terrible place to live in. It's dark and scary in there.

THE THIRTEEN COMMANDMENTS

1. Don't be your mother. Or Anderson Cooper. Or your cat.

2. Chill.

3. Party hard.

4. Shop 'til you drop.

5. Don't get mad. Get even. Or odd.

6. Rant, then lighten up.

7. Sleep when you're dead.

8. Kvetch.

9. Easy come, easy go.

10. A good stew can be satisfying.

11. Que sera sera.

12. Fun is not a four-letter word.

13. There's only salami on rye.

If you understand any of these cockamamie commandments, please explain them to me.

OH GOODY, ANOTHER QUIZ!
WHAT IS THE ORIGIN OF YOUR MISERY?

Read the following statements and check the ones that ring true for you.

___ I have low-esteem not only for myself but for others.

___ The dire human condition disturbs my metabolism.

___ The world is upside down, and I have motion sickness.

___ I'm always on a deprivation diet.

___ I'm sleepless in Seattle.

___ Poor potty training dogs me to this day.

___ World peace is elusive as ever.

___ I choose to identify as a Kardashian. Where's *my* money?

___ The weather is wacky.

___ My favorite TV show was cancelled.

___ Deep in my heart... it's cold in there!

___ My inner child mocks me.

___ I'm fresh out of chocolate.

___ I'm awake in Seattle.

___ The pulsating zit on my nose is scaring the dog.

___ I have a fear of flying in the middle coach seat.

___ It's been a bad hair month.

___ The cat p-whips me day and night.

___ My tennis backhand sucks.

___ The internet is too damn slow.

SCORING: If you checked 15–20 statements TRUE, you're morbidly honest. Don't get out of bed tomorrow morning.

If you checked 10–15 as TRUE, you're average. Sorry, nobody's gonna throw a pity party for you.

If you checked 9 or fewer as TRUE, you're in glorious denial of reality. Awesome strategy!

If you put Xs instead of checks, you get an A for creativity but an F for not following directions, which equals a sad C. You have a great future as an entrepreneur or an anger management counselor.

How to Avoid Selfie Suicide

We know it's all about you, you, you, BUT . . .

Some selfies simply aren't worth snapping.

It's high time smartphones come with warning labels!

1. Don't climb on top of a speeding train to take a daring selfie. This only works well in high-budget action movies. You. Will. Die. Horribly.

2. Don't snap a selfie of you and your cute, little dog kissing while driving at 70 miles per hour on the five-lane freeway. You might as well let the dog drive—even if he has been drinking.

3. It is not a great idea to pose near "the edge" of anything, and especially when live electrical wires are within striking distance.

4. Best not to take a selfie while committing a crime or posing with stolen goods. Cell phones are *really* expensive in the pokey.

5. Please! No selfies with loaded guns, flaming torches, wild animals, or poisonous snakes. Trust me. This will not end well. The world will assume you are a total moron and laugh mercilessly at your foolhardy demise. Can you blame them?

6. If you are married, do not stage a sexy selfie with your girlfriend, boyfriend, or pet goat. It will come back to "byte" you in the wallet.

7. If you encounter a desperate individual perched precariously on a high bridge who is threatening to leap to his icy death any second . . . it may *not* be the optimal time for a giddy selfie hello from you. This reminds me of the oddly empowered folks who wave maniacally behind reporters on live television broadcast feeds.

8. Taking selfies with your drunken frat bros and a sex doll at Ground Zero? Not cool.

AFFIRMATIONS FOR THE SELF-ABSORBED

- Me, me, me is my mantra.
- I feel therefore I am.
- I believe in the power of panache and pralines.
- Self-Love is my BFF.
- God bless the camera on my cellphone.
- I spoil my inner child with effusive compliments.

THE LITANY OF FUN

and then we got on the bus and then we all had treats and then we sang songs and then we played games and then Billy and Kenny got into a fight over a Ninja and then we got off the bus and then we had a snack and then we stood in line and then we got tickets and then we went into the zoo and then we saw the Wild Africa exhibit and then we got back in line and then we saw the Hall of Bats exhibit and then we were talking and laughing and then we got back in line and then Mrs. Hudson got mad at us and then we got quieter and then we marched to the picnic tables and then we sat down and then some of us got hot dogs at the concession stand and then some of us got burgers with cheese and some of us got burgers without cheese and then we ate lunch and then we got back in line and then we went to the Wild World of Monkeys and then we went to Our Undersea Friends and then Mrs. Hudson yelled at us some more and then we had a snack under a tree and then we got back in line and then we went to the souvenir shop and then we bought monkey stickers or erasers that had bat heads or T-shirts that said "I've Been to Herkimer Zoo" or key chains with little whales hanging from them and then we walked back to Parking Lot B and then we got on the bus and then Mr. Jones drove us home and here I am

R. Chast

SEPTEMBER

LITTLE MONSTERS

"Insanity is hereditary; you get it from your children."
—SAM LEVENSON

Back to school, back to work, and best of all, back to competitive parenting. Start your engines, helicopter parents.

Vroom. Vroom.

FLIGHT LOG OF A HELICOPTER MOM

- *6:00 a.m.* Strength train for endurance. Focus on flabby upper-body muscles. Remind self that helicopter parenting is an ultramarathon, not a cakewalk for wimps.

THE MISERY MANIFESTO

- *6:30 a.m.* Fuel up at Starbuck's on a tall quadruple espresso roast, komodo dragon blend—no milk, no sugar, no cup.

- *7:00 a.m.* Drill preadolescent kids with calculus and chemistry flashcards over omega-3 rich, low-fructose breakfasts. Tell them, "Bone up; those AP courses are right around the corner."

- *7:30 a.m.* Drop off sweet, attention-challenged male child and intense, snarky female child at middle school with detailed instructions for the entire day.

- *8:00 a.m.* Check female child's social media profiles. Post anonymous grandiose compliments to improve her body image and boost core self-esteem.

- *8:30 a.m.* Install filter on male child's laptop so those "naughty thong girls acting wild and wet" websites don't inexplicably pop up again on his favorites list.

- *9:01 a.m.* Answer call from whining school principal upset with male child's "inappropriate" lunchtime behavior. Listen politely; threaten multiple lawsuits and 911 calls to the ACLU and *HuffPost*. (Make note to confiscate said child's pocket video camera.)

- *9:30 a.m.* Crank up on personal stash of putrid herbal energy supplements since hovering requires continuous, active course corrections from the pilot.

- *10:00 a.m.* Call male child's cell phone. Leave firm message that "appreciating the female gender" doesn't include filming the morbidly obese school librarian straining in the teachers' lounge, then posting it on YouTube. Geez, what will Harvard think?

- *10:30 a.m.* Drop by schoolyard at snack time and nudge female child, thus aggravating both your eating disorders. "Are you savoring your vegetables? Remember, broccoli is brain food . . . and it's slimming, too."

- *11:00 a.m.* At biweekly appointment, ask therapist to define *hover*. Deny lack of stability 'til the friggin' malevolent, methane-emitting cows come home.

- *12:00 p.m.* Fuel up on iced mocha double double espresso Frappuccino Gazebo Blend with cumin sprinkles and whipped cream. Top off with a scrumptious giant cherry apricot scone for extra lift.

- *12:30 p.m.* Incessant helicopter din and teeth-rattling vibration grating on already rattled nerves. Get lube job and mani-pedi at tacky day spa. Have mechanic sharpen motor blades and check torque tension.

- *1:55 p.m.* Ignore slacker husband's remark, "Duh. Why do you think they call it *hell*icopter?"

- *2:00 p.m.* Do research for female child's science project on hummingbirds and the physics of flight. You gotta earn those A's, they don't grow on trees—especially on our family tree!

- *2:45 p.m.* Call female child's English teacher and berate her for that B on the *Macbeth* essay last week.

- *2:55 p.m.* Call male child on cell phone and insist he text you his score on that afternoon's spelling test *now*. Excellence waits for no one.

- *3:00 p.m.* Call therapist. Demand she clarify "*too* involved." Disagree vehemently and vow innocence 'til Iceland melts off the geothermal map.

- *3:15 p.m.* Detect ominous downward spiral at accelerating speed. Panic creeps in.

- *3:16 p.m.* Reflect on therapist's comment that "helicopters are very unstable; hovering is like balancing yourself while standing on a large beach ball."

- *3:17 p.m.* Chopper pitches and rolls like a drunken windmill. "Holy F#@*!!"

- *3:18 p.m.* Tear up parent card and toss pilot wings in the trash.

- *3:19 p.m.* Prepare for a crash landing as fuel abruptly runs out. View is entirely obscured by stress-induced, adrenaline-juiced brain fog.

- *3:20 p.m.* Collapse at cyclic switch; kiss your asinine aspirations adieu as your chopper shakes to a million bits in midair.

- *3:21 p.m.* Plummet to a sure death of regret and many broken bones but land miraculously... in an empty nest.

- *3:33 p.m.* Vegetate there while deviant male child and dour female child learn to fly on their own two feet and perhaps someday in the distant future elect to conduct a search and rescue mission for you, their Top Mom.

TOP TEN COUNTRY SONGS FOR THE BELEAGUERED

Being a parent can be tedious. You're overwhelmed with a multitude of tasks and concerns. You often feel stressed and down in the dumps. It's time to get out your ukulele and harmonica and take a music break. Sing along, and encourage the dog to bay with you!

1. "The Terrible Twos Are Givin' Me the Blues"

2. "We're All Unhappy Campers on This Road Trip in Life"

3. "Those Cool Moms Are Gettin' Me Hot"

4. "Achy Breaky Bank Account"

5. "If Mamma Ain't Mellow, Ain't Nobody Mellow"

6. "The More You Whine, the More I Wine"

7. "Wholesome Prison Blues"

8. "Stand by Your Man-Child"

9. "Don't Let Your Babies Grow Up to Be Lawyers"

10. "Crazy! I Love You, but You're Driving Me Crazy!"

COLLEGE SURVIVAL 101 FOR HELICOPTER KIDS

How the heck are you going to survive that first heart-wrenching, nut-grinding year away from home sweet home and your helicopter mommy? Here are 10 tough love tips.

1. **COOL IT.** Get over yourself already. You're not dying. You're not even sick, drama queen. Your time watching TV at home will merely be interrupted by a series of three-week stretches where you'll be forced to crash in subpar housing, share critically dirty bathrooms with other poor schlubs, and occasionally fake a passion for (ugh!) higher learning.

2. **DEVELOP AN ADDICTION TO THAT FINE, WHITE MIRACLE POWDER—CAFFEINE.** Forget those cheesy radio alarm clocks. Dragging your sorry ass up in the cold, dark morn is easier when you're dependent on coffee and *must* pull yourself up, crawl outside, stumble to the nearest Starbucks, and slam that crippling withdrawal migraine with a stiff cup of high-octane Joe. Addiction is a real motivator.

3. **REMEMBER, SLEEP IS OVERRATED.** Don't be a baby about getting "enough" sleep. A sign of true maturity is realizing there's *no* such thing as "enough." (Think sex, money, happiness, Twinkies.) Anyway, you can always nap during your coma-inducing classes. It's common knowledge that the last ten rows in lecture halls are specifically designed for this purpose. Remember, one of the perks of college life is having *no* bedtime and actually *wanting* to stay up all night playing Candy Crush.

4. **EAT EVERYTHING IN SIGHT.** Why not? It's easy. The chow is covered by your meal plan, you don't have to break a sweat to hunt it down, plus there's nobody there to nag you about bingeing! Snacking is an entertaining hobby and, if you cultivate it with enthusiasm, a twenty-four-hour activity. So what if you're chronically constipated and your jeans have holes in all the wrong places? Go ahead! Graze lustily at those gargantuan all-you-can-gorge buffets. Pig out at the cupcake and cookie study breaks. Don't fret over gaining the freshman twenty—if you're an average teenager, you're probably already twenty-five, thirty pounds overweight anyway . . . so what's another forty?

5. **GET THE FACTS.** The facts of life, of course. If you aspire to be a campus Romeo, better rev up that pea brain of yours for prophylactic news you can use. Learn the basics of birth control (abstinence), symptoms of STDs, and essential sexting acronyms, then jot them on your sweaty palm for quick reference.

6. **OPEN WIDE.** You'll be exposed (obscenely, at times) to TMI, idea pollution, mind-boggling nerds, pathological preppies, ultrasophisticated and otherworldly

views, and freaks you wouldn't accept a blood donation from if you were croaking from a vampire attack. (See course catalog, student handbook, class profile.) Get your pooper-scooper ready; it's a daily drive-by dumping of tiresome information.

7. **MEET WITH YOUR PROFESSORS.** Especially the few reasonably young, horny ones. Nail a one-on-one session in that remote office off campus to pontificate on your intellectual passions. Hold your nose, bring an overpriced bottle of French wine, and kiss butt like crazy. This is excellent practice for dating in the real world later. And you never know, something positive could come from this tedious chore—can you spell "sexual harassment settlement?" *Ka-ching!*

8. **PLEDGING.** Lie, cheat, steal, bribe, and offer unsavory favors to get into a fraternity. *Any* fraternity will do, and the wilder the better. Think of the sterling role models you'll be exposed to, the rock band of bros you'll bond with. Where else can you learn how to guzzle six-packs of beer; hold your hard liquor; offend nice girls, older women, and chipmunks; and, best of all, score with superskanks? Plus you may finally experience something you never felt in five years of high school: a trace of popularity. Relish it. It's fleeting.

9. **HYGIENE.** There are basic hygiene facts you'll come to appreciate. You can easily go a whole year (or at least a semester) without washing your clothes. Nobody cares. Nobody will even notice. BTW, one shower a month is sufficient. Everyone stinks anyway. Deodorant causes cancer and shampoo is a waste of money—money you could be spending on caffeine. Remember: greasy hair is happy hair.

10. **REPEAT THE FOLLOWING AFFIRMATION.** "I didn't die, I'm just away, I didn't die, I'm just away." (And never forget . . . Mommy and Daddy are a mere speed dial away on their cells!)

HOW TO GET YOUR KID TO GO GREEN AT COLLEGE

As an upstanding global citizen, you'll feel the need to instruct your prodigy to be ecominded and environmentally responsible at school. This will impress their college administrators more than a brilliant intellect or a mastery of critical thinking. Be sure to share these green tips with them.

1. **GRAZE** on 100 percent organic veggie soy wheat grass. So what if this faux food tastes as disgusting as it smells and costs more than a carton of Twinkies? Your skin will turn a cool shade of sour apple that will demonstrate to all who are checking—especially your cute professors—that you're pro-green.

2. **RECYCLE** your impressive collection of lite beer, Cherry Coke, Dr. Pepper, and Red Bull cans. FYI—container waste is *not* a design choice.

3. **RIDE A BIKE** instead of driving a car. This may save the planet from toxic gas emissions and really annoying cataclysmic global warming. What fun you'll have pushing the pedals through five feet of snow and ice in single-digit temperatures and gale-force winds.

THE MISERY MANIFESTO

4. **DITCH THE MICROWAVE.** *No* midnight popcorn breaks or breakfast burritos for you. No nuking is good nuking, Orville Redenbacher and Jimmy Dean be damned. Besides, corn kernels are desperately needed for ethanol conversion.

5. **SHOWER** with complete strangers, or better yet, skip that shower! Nobody will care; everybody smells funky at college.

6. **KEEP A PET GOAT** in your dorm room to manage tiresome housekeeping tasks. This will eliminate the need for garbage pickups. In addition, toilet training your four-legged, hundred-pound buddy can be an exciting adventure for both of you. Benefit: It never hurts to have a hairy friend on long winter nights. Life away from home can be oh so lonely.

7. **WIND POWER.** Convert your professors' interminable lectures into wind power by surreptitiously hooking them up to your genius roommate's advanced eco-bio-tech-engineering class project.

8. **TURN THE THERMOSTAT WAY DOWN.** If the climate gods had meant for you to be warm and cozy, they would've given you a dense, matted coat of animal fur—or better yet, a girl or boyfriend.

9. **MAKE YOUR OWN CLOTHES.** Cuts down on the toxic chemicals used in manufacturing normal, store-bought clothes. No sewing knowledge is necessary—duct tape, staples, and dumpsters scraps will do the trick. So what if you look like an agoraphobic from an incestuous religious cult?

10. **PROPELLER HAT.** Propeller beanies are a viable (albeit humble) form of windmill power. Wear yours proudly. They're fast becoming a staple of the serious advocate's wardrobe.

AFFIRMATIONS FOR PARENTS

- A toddler's incessant scream is music to my ears.
- I will not cry over spilled milk, juice, soda, coffee, tea, wine, or Scotch.
- Sleepless nights drain me of all sexual desire.
- A slim, confident body I shall never know again.
- My personal hygiene is not a priority.
- Elephants and kids never forget.

OCTOBER

TECHNOLOGY HELL

"Misery's fine—as long as you know
you can get out of it when you want to."

—ARTHUR ADAMOV

BYTE ME

Your smartphone has a case that reads: "I'm with Stupid."

TECHNOLOGY WILL KILL US ALL

If technology doesn't kill us, it won't make us stronger. It'll bankrupt us by making us spend a fortune on brain scans and the latest, newer, better smartphones.

TEXT NECK

We're evolving into a race of hunchbacks. The younger you are, the worse your hump. Quasimodo, eat your heart out.

CARPAL TUNNEL SYNDROME

Ouch. Thanks to my time on the keyboard, I can no longer open a plastic water bottle or zip my fly without wincing in pain.

INTERNET ADDICTION

Who says you can't get too much of a good thing? Lights, camera, rehab!

REQUIEM FOR A PACK RAT: HELP! I'M A DATA HOARDER

Someday, most likely sooner than later, my lovely yet unwitting neighbors will find me buried in a heap of festering digital clutter. It will be a death trap of epic proportions.

My final resting place will be a cyber landfill of multimedia content that I tragically couldn't resist. Help! I'm a data hoarder.

I will forever slumber among the Twitter droppings, Pinterest images, Yahoo postings, Facebook photos, and Digg mounds of must-read articles on cool parenting, anti-aging tricks, essential super foods, red velvet cake recipes, belly fat exercises, cosmetic surgery ads, book chat, pet dander warnings, extreme coupons, and titillating celebrity drivel.

I'll be shrink-wrapped in a shroud of utterly fascinating emails, rib-tickling blog posts, captivating audio, eBooks, podcasts, PDFs, JPEGs, GIFs, and irresistible YouTube videos of nursing puppies, witty cats, and pea-brained humans. Zip files of fashion and style tips I'll never be tall enough, thin enough, young enough, or rich enough to open will haunt my eternal soul.

Whoever said knowledge is power didn't have twenty-four-seven wireless connectivity, Google, and a 5.O GHz processor. I'll never excavate myself from this morass of oversharing and endless connecting.

My whopping addiction to—not Vodka martinis or Camel Lights—but collecting information will cause my downfall. It will be death by a thousand billion clicks.

I'm not alone. Like many, I suffer from OCDD: Obsessive-Compulsive Data Disorder. Compounded by an attachment issue to TMI (too much information), this pretty much makes me a pack rat on steroids.

This buildup of useless information is obstructing blood flow to my brain and curtailing my circulation in the real world. Forget about clogged arteries—I need to clear the plaque from my hard drive!

I know what you're thinking. Perhaps with therapy, support, generous doses of chocolate, serious begging from disgruntled relatives, and a U-Haul truck full of super patient professional organizers who are happily billing by the hour, I can clean up my act before I byte the—Oh no, chest pains! My vision is blurry! My cheeks (all four of them) are numb!

Uh, oh . . . I'm having a computer stroke. The Grim Reaper is tormenting me: "Ha ha! It's too late to reduce, reuse, and recycle."

Farewell, my friends, and one final request: stop, drop, and delete.

I can see my epitaph now:

Here I lay (or is it lie?),
Buried alive by TMI.

CUT THE CORD

I confess, I can't cut the cord. At last count, I am possessed by a collection of ninety-five cords. These include charger cords to phones I no longer own, electrical cords to devices that have gone the way of my wasted youth, and connection cords to iPods, iPads, and iMacs I no longer have relationships with. I don't own a junk drawer; I own a junk dresser. Several, actually. Seriously. I have enough cords to hold a mass cult suicide by hanging.

"Why keep them?" you ask. It's because I'm a saver. I toss nothing device-related out. What if someone needs one of these cords someday? I, alone, will have it. I'll be able to rescue them from their despair. (Admittedly, it occurs to me that *I* may be the one who needs it.)

Trying to keep up with new gadgets and their accompanying cords and cables is like playing hopscotch on quicksand. How can we feel secure with technology when it changes every two months? So, for the time being, I'll save the cords—all of them. Hey, it's not my fault! People have always said I'm a keeper.

I INK, THEREFORE I AM

Once upon a time, long, long ago . . . there was the telephone.

It was a genteel instrument of communication on a rubberized spiral cord that appeared at restaurant tables only on rare occasion, accorded exclusively to A-list movie stars at the Polo Lounge or, if global crisis demanded it, the president of the United States.

Today, it's a plague on civilized society. This is an issue we must no longer sweep under the placemat like errant breadcrumbs. Cell phone etiquette, especially in restaurants, is an oxymoron. Pray tell, what is "smart" about a phone that destroys *direct* human interaction?

Yes, the omnipresence of cellular technology is a curse on us poor fools who archaically cling to common courtesy. Like the Hansen Writing Ball, the private conversation is a thing of the past. We're now forced to be involved with mankind—often as voyeurs.

Imagine you're seated at a fine dining establishment with a business colleague or appealing social acquaintance. You're anticipating a pleasant experience. But no! Your companion brings out his cell and rudely starts chatting and/or texting God knows what to God knows who.

This boorish behavior is both vexing and embarrassing. It's more irritating than bawling babies and cackling rug rats running amuck. For God's sake, if I wanted to cultivate bleeding ulcers and chronic acid reflux, I'd eat more meals at home with my contentious spouse, raucous ankle-biters, and yapping dog.

I assume you, like me, resent this exasperating intrusion on your sparkling repartee. So, what's a gentleman (or gentle lady) to do?

Protecting your sanity will no doubt be an onerous challenge in personal discipline and rage management. First, you must quell that overwhelming urge to grasp your shrimp fork, pounce on the offender, and puncture him like an overcooked rump roast. You can stare daggers at him and try to tough it out, but beware of your blood pressure, as this strategy will further rankle your nerves. Instead,

- Draw your electronic weapon of choice and immerse yourself in a lengthy game of Sudoku or Text Twist.

- Lob buttered dinner rolls at the SOB.

- Sigh loudly enough to be heard in the kitchen.

- Ask the waiter for crayons and summon your inner Picasso.

- Whip out the mint-flavored Glide and commence flossing.

- Whistle an annoying tune. (Anything by Miley Cyrus will do.)

- Create an explosive concoction with the condiments on the table.

- Resist the tendency to transform your tedium into sexual fantasy, as you'll most likely become discombobulated and spill your cocktail all over your freshly pressed linen pants.

- Bellow statistics from the latest alarming study that links the use of cell phones to brain cancer.

If all else fails, ask the manager to post the following warning: "The use of cell phones will result in their immediate confiscation and your prompt annihilation by a ravenous wood chipper."

Ask not for whom the cell tolls—it tolls for thee.

CHECK THIS OUT

Do you despise using those self-checkout machines in grocery stores as much as I do? They're the ones where you scan your own items, bag them, and pay with a computer keypad.

Excuse me, but isn't this the checker's job? You know, the one who's lurking outside the store entrance smoking a cigarette and yakking mindlessly on her cell phone? If I'm going to check out my overpriced items myself, I demand medical insurance, a dental plan, and an employee discount.

Consumers, unite! We may need to unionize.

AFFIRMATIONS FOR THE TECHNOLOGY TORTURED

- Guilt and remorse stalk me like a fake Facebook friend.

- Smiley faces and sappy emoticons piss me off.

- I am down with the Internet.

- I am a magnet for all the misery online.

- My computer is not too slow. I am too slow.

- Even my selfies sneer at me.

NOVEMBER

SLOTH

"There is no such thing as fun for the whole family."
—JERRY SEINFELD

STUFFED

The media messages are loud and clear: Eat, drink, and be merry—or else!

Holiday food is highly entertaining in its presentation and variety. It's a temptation few of us can resist.

Gluttony is a great pleasure if you learn to lose the guilt. Pecan pie, hazelnut stuffing, yam soufflé, and turkey legs with gravy . . . will kill you if you do it right. Who needs crack cocaine or a stool softener when you've got Grandma's infamous rum-laced eggnog?

My advice: Knock yourself out on holiday party food. Go. To. Town. Remember, the family that binges like nobody is watching is the family that shares cardiac disease together. So indulge. There's always time for a pumpkin detox and lemon juice cleanse later.

DO THE MISERY MATH

Overindulgence has consequences.

ATTITUDE: DOES YOURS SUCK?

Answer "Damn Right" or "Never":

1. Do you get angry at the drop of a sombrero?
2. Do you try to control what you can't control?
3. Do you insist on being right all the time?
4. Do you part your hair down the middle?
5. Do you blame others for your misfortune?
6. Do you constantly compare yourself to others?

7. Do you fear success more than failure?

8. Do you eat your feelings? Do they taste like chicken?

If you answered "Damn Right" to four or more questions, you're a nudnik. Stop letting your inner critic bully you. You're likely to succumb to a substance addiction any minute.

If you answered "Never" to four or more questions, you're in deep denial. You're likely to succumb to a process addiction any second.

THE TOOTH HURTS

I saw a billboard recently that advertised "total sleep dentistry." On it was an exceptionally hot young blonde (is there any other kind?) wearing a red polka-dot bikini (or was it a thong with spandex pasties?) and a glistening smile. Her blinding whites radiated like a sparkling, 3D movie star's, as if they'd been stroked not by a toothbrush but Tinkerbell's magic wand.

The giant plug in the sky obscuring my sunlight and scenic view promised *no* pain, *no* memory, *no* suffering—*no* lie!

Whew! Talk about promises, promises! No lie? Forget about our paltry plebeian fibs: "The refund check is in the mail," "I texted you to cancel the wedding, didn't you get it?" "So sorry, the computers have been down in the dumps all morning," and my personal fave, "Big deal, I'm five hours late. There was traffic."

Cross your heart and hope to die (effortlessly, of course)—you'll have *no* pain during the usual emotional and physical torture of being pinned down in an unattractive faux leather dentist chair while highly sensitive and personal parts of your piehole are summarily cut, gouged, scraped, and excavated.

Guess we can kiss "no pain, no gain" good-bye. If innovation and technology can bring us the glorious benefits of fully sedated dentistry, then perhaps there are no limits. How about no-pain adolescence, total-sleep marriage, no-memory divorce, no-anguish parenting, no-suffering funerals, and carefree chemo?

You decide: no lie or no life? Either way, a honking dose of laughing gas is always welcome in my daily slogfest of trials and tribulations.

LAST-DITCH IDEAS: HOW TO BE HAPPIER

Remember to enjoy the positive, however infinitesimal, and the good, however scarce.

- Build a shrine to Mr. Peanut.

- Change your gender. Hey, worth a try.

- Be more than you can be: have yourself cloned.

- Change that boring hairstyle you've been sporting for fifty years.

- Swap religions with a friend.

- Donate some organs.

- Take a robot to lunch.

- Learn to play the accordion and see who your friends *really* are.

- Go cold turkey on veggies—NO green vegetables for a week.

- Eat like you have five days to live.

- Strut around with a tight t-shirt that says, "Old people know where to put it."

- Smile weirdly at strangers for the heck of it.

PAIN IS UNIVERSAL

The Universal Pain Assessment Tool is an excellent gauge for monitoring family members' stress levels during the Thanksgiving meal. That which we measure, we can medicate.

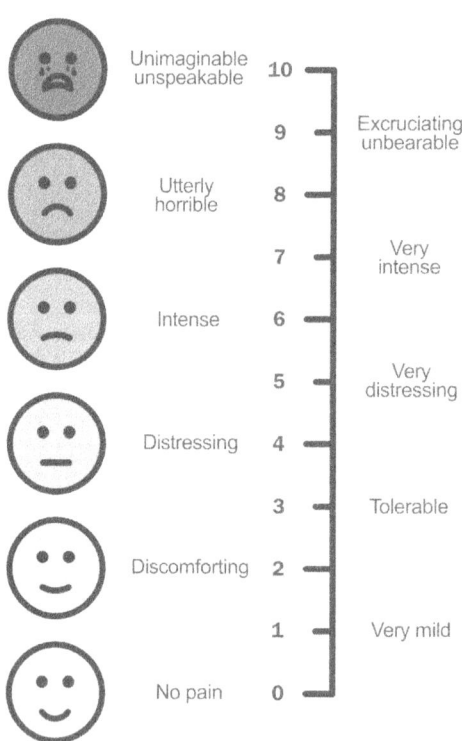

- Those fortunate to be experiencing "No Pain" are either under the age of five or drunk. They certainly aren't listening to Uncle Frank proselytize about politics, and they damn sure aren't doing the cooking.

- Let's face it: Anyone with "Mild Pain" or "Moderate Pain" can be ignored. They're not serious contenders in the competition for attention. Expression of distress is a family sport these slackers obviously don't appreciate.

- Those with "Severe Pain" are in it to win it. Their slow blinks and open mouths are accompanied by lots of impressive groaning. We *all* feel their pain.

- Please note that with "Worst Pain Possible," bed rest is required. Make sure you have enough sleeping surfaces on hand for all your holiday guests. Most likely, by the end of the meal, your dear relatives will be experiencing unbearable misery and need to crash. Go, team!

AFFIRMATIONS FOR THE GRATITUDE CHALLENGED

- I am rich like a crème donut is rich.
- I feel the love of small, smelly animals.
- I am grateful that Hitler is dead.
- I am grateful for the moon and the stars and the cocoa bean.
- I am grateful for the kindly stink bug.
- I am grateful for readers who buy books, especially mine.

DECEMBER

XTREME STRESS

"No matter how cynical you become,
it's never enough to keep up."

—LILY TOMLIN

ROYALLY SCROOGED

Nothing says grace under pressure like holiday stress. It's in these dark days of trial and turmoil that you'll be tested. Your mettle will be put to the pedal.

The wackadoos will come out of the woodwork. Some will be neighbors. Some will be family. Some will be friends. Many will be insane.

It will be your job to contain the crazy, preferably without firearms and cops.

HOLIDAYS ARE A PAIN IN THE ASPIRATIONS

You'd like peace and quiet for the holidays. You want to relax. You want to stop and inhale the roses. You're sadly optimistic on this count.

Instead, you'll be busier than ever. Holidays require an inordinate amount of energy and time. You have stuff to do you didn't know you had to do. Even if you're taking a week off from work, you'll be busting your ass big-time. *Ho, ho, ho!*

A QUIZ: WILL YOU SURVIVE THE HOLIDAYS?

1. When you hear "ho, ho, ho," you . . .

    a. Break out in hives
    b. Assume Uncle Jerry is drunk again
    c. Feel a dark cloud moving over you
    d. Remember you're late paying your Visa bill
    e. Are warmed by the holiday spirit

2. Your aging mother calls and insists you help her with her chirpy annual Christmas tea party. You . . .

    a. Fake mononucleosis to avoid the tiresome event

b. Book a one-way ticket to Bora Bora
c. Pick a nasty fight with Mom so she won't speak to you for a couple of years
d. Rent a female sibling so she can deal with it
e. Stock up on Xanax and feign holiday cheer one last time

3. You have no time in December to work on a committee because . . .

   a. You're trying to decide if you've been naughty or nice
   b. You're revising your annual holiday letter for maximum impact
   c. You're busy recycling Christmas gifts from last year
   d. Those damn gingerbread houses keep collapsing
   e. You're making out under the mistletoe

4. On the first day of Christmas your true love gave to you . . .

   a. Nothing. He's a minimalist.
   b. A pear in a partridge tree. He's dyslexic.
   c. Two turtle doves. He can't count.
   d. Enough germs to wipe out a kindergarten class
   e. The caress and smile of an angel

5. The holidays fill you with . . .

   a. Anxiety
   b. Gas

c. High cholesterol
d. Flashbacks
e. Unbearable joy

SCORING: If you answered A–D on any of the questions, brace yourself for a bumpy yuletide. If you chose E on any of the questions, you own too many Christmas sweaters.

CREATE NEW FAMILY TRADITIONS

Holidays are a golden opportunity to make lasting memories and create new traditions for generations to come. This is also an opportunity to solidify your legacy and control your spawn from the grave.

- Start a ritual of Christmas karaoke. Beats Christmas caroling door to door in the bitter cold. After a couple of hours, you'll beg for "Silent Night."

- Run out and get "Santa Baby" tattoos for everyone in the family. Grandma will love her fanny one.

- Refresh your cookie-baking regimen by skipping the baking part: Decorate and serve blobs of raw cookie dough. This not only tastes better but also saves valuable time and energy for drinking.

- Decorate the Christmas tree naked. (You, not the tree.)

- Remember, the cat needs some fun, too. So don't forget to dress up the dog in a goofball sweater, reindeer antlers, a red clown nose, and faux icicles. Top him off with garlands of buttered popcorn. This inanity provides hours of hilarity for all, plus it's a priceless photo opp.

- Give your gift giving a contemporary twist: Instead of the ho-hum wrapping of presents and placing them under the tree, hide them around the house. What fun it will be to dig your diamond earrings out of the dirty laundry hamper!

- Hold an annual happy holidays food fight. What better way to use unclaimed gingerbread boys, marshmallow snowmen, cheese balls, date rolls, dried apricots, peppermint bark, and—God forbid someone sent you some—Moose Munch?

- How 'bout a novel twist on the holiday fruitcake that makes the rounds every year? Nothing says "Ho, Ho, Ho" like a death in the family. For instance, when I die, I'd like to be cremated and have my ashes baked into a fruitcake, which can then be recycled among loved ones at Christmastime forever—you've got mail. ☺

HOLIDAY GIFTS I DON'T WANT

Gone are the days when you were a little tyke who scribbled down a list of toys you wanted for Christmas. You mailed your request to Santa Claus, and Mom usually delivered. It's more complicated now, isn't it?

The holiday gifts I don't want:

- Absolutely nothing handmade or concocted, unless you're a three-year-old who doesn't have your own credit card yet.

- No personal hygiene products. This includes the usual suspects: nose hair trimmer, butt firmer, calf wax, electric eyebrow plucker, and miracle aging cream.

- No Christmas or Hanukkah decorations. A gift you can only use for one week a year inherently lacks charm.

- Gag gifts—except perhaps for the singing, dancing plastic fish on the plaque. We must recognize great talent when we see it.

- Cheap wine. Life is too short.

- Recycled food gifts. Who ya kiddin' with that f-ing fruitcake?

- Anything that requires batteries (yes, even a vibrator).

- Anything that says, "assembly needed." For obvious reasons.

Instead of wedding registries, maybe we should all sign up for holiday registries. Perhaps then we'll actually get what we want.

WHIZDOM OF THE AGES

Happiness should not be a J-O-B.

Sometimes a rainbow is just a rainbow and not a sign that unicorns are blowing you air kisses.

Radical "happiness projects" are sure to depress the crap out of you.

Every party has a pooper. That's why they invited you.

Remember the unconditional love that's coming your way now. It won't last.

If you're one happiness book away from blowing your brains out, maybe you should try medication rather than an endless to-do list.

Middle-aged women who constantly exclaim "Zoikes!" "Whammo!" and "Gee Whiz!" grate on people's nerves.

The days are long . . . and some self-help books are even longer.

Yes, Virginia, a personal trainer and a weekly massage can make you happier. Keep dreamin'!

If you don't have a lot of money to buy happiness, try leasing.

A Caterpillar crane can't lift your mood as high as a carnival-size bucket of warm kettle corn.

Reincarnation = same clowns, different circus.

GOOD NEWS: This year is almost over.

BAD NEWS: Next year has (almost) begun.

AFFIRMATIONS FOR THE FRAZZLED

- My nerves jingle jangle like cowbells in an earthquake.

- I am enough, and I set the bar low.

- I'd rather have the insides of my eyelids waxed than "get serious about silly."

- I am destined to be lost in the spam file of life.

- The Universe conspires to ignore my deepest wishes.

- I pray for peace on Earth and Pluto.

CONCLUSION

THE MISERY MANIFESTO

To be happy—or at the least less miserable—don't think.

The days are long, but the years are even longer. And the decades? Blech!

If you truly want to be miserable, recite this masochistic little rhyme fifty times a day:

"Good, better, best.
Never let it rest.
Until your good is better,
And your better is best."

POINTS TO PONDER:

- Happiness is chocolate, but chocolate isn't happiness.
- War is hell. So is dieting.
- It's my pity party and I'll post a crying selfie if I want to.
- A messy car makes a cozy home away from home.
- Comfort foods are a gift from God.
- Deprivation sucks. Try to avoid it.
- Life is not a multiple-choice test. It's a pop quiz graded on a curve.
- You must be the happiness you seek.
- Don't count your chickens before the fat lady sings for her supper.
- An orgasm in the hand is worth two in the bush.
- The opposite of work isn't play. It's more work.
- It's a basic truth that the body doesn't lie. It lays.
- A crooked smile is better than uncontrolled crying.

THE MISERY MANIFESTO

- Other people's radical happiness projects are most likely a desperate cry for help.

- When the Bluebird of Happiness flies smack into the picture window, it becomes the Black-and-Blue Bird of Unhappiness.

- Embrace tomfoolery as if it were a rich relative on his deathbed.

- Namaste to all and to all a good night.

ABOUT THE AUTHOR

Barb Best feels your pain. Her comedy material has been performed by Joan Rivers and published in numerous print and online publications. Her humor blog appears on Guy Kawasaki's Alltop Best of the Best site, alongside the *Bloggess*, *McSweeney's*, and the *Onion*. She is honored to be an Erma Bombeck Global Humor Winner and a Robert Benchley Society Humor Writing Top Ten Winner. Barb supports humor healthcare non-profits the Association of Applied & Therapeutic Humor, Rx Laughter, and ComedyCures.

Subscribe to her popular blog I Feel Your Pain! at BarbBest.com and feel the joy.

BUT WAIT! THERE'S MORE!

ALSO AVAILABLE AS EBOOKS ON AMAZON

Find Your Funny: A Survival Guide for Teens

100 Fast & Funny: Ha-Musings

Smiles To Go: Take-Out for the ☺ Hungry

ANTHOLOGIES

My Funny Valentine

My Funny Major Medical

Your Glasses Are On Top of Your Head

FOR INFORMATION ABOUT DISCOUNTS ON BULK PURCHASES, CONTACT BARBSBLAST@GMAIL.COM

www.ingramcontent.com/pod-product-compliance
Lightning Source LLC
Chambersburg PA
CBHW080519300426
44112CB00018B/2797